Big
Jesus

Big
Jesus

A Pastor's Struggle with Christology

Jimmy R. Watson

WIPF & STOCK · Eugene, Oregon

BIG JESUS
A Pastor's Struggle with Christology

Wipf & Stock
An Imprint of Wipf and Stock Publishers
199 W. 8th Ave., Suite 3
Eugene, OR 97401

www.wipfandstock.com

ISBN 13: 978-1-4982-0048-6

Manufactured in the U.S.A.

This book is dedicated to my dog, children, step-children, grandchildren, parents, grandparents, siblings, in-laws, nephews, nieces, friends, parishioners, stalkers, Mexican food restaurants, Jesus,

and my wife
—a beautiful, artistic, special needs advocate and future Roman Catholic woman priest.

Thanks, Annie, for locking the door until I finished writing.

Contents

Preface

I DECIDED TO WRITE a book about Jesus for two reasons. First, I thought people might be interested. Not that I am motivated by royalties; however, there does seem to be a lot of passion about Jesus books. I googled "list of books about Jesus" and discovered a bibliography that exceeds even the discography of REM's music. I can't think of another human being, at least not in my neck of the woods, who stirs as much passion, creates as many communities in his name—albeit fragmented beyond his wildest imagination—and inspires as many wannabe authors, artists, dancers, orators, and those who hope the world will end in a flaming ball of glory, as Jesus.

The second reason I decided to write a book about Jesus is because I looked around, followed my shadow for a few days, asked myself probing questions, conferred with dead relatives, and made the startling discovery that my greatest passion since about 1981 has focused on the first-century long-haired, dark-skinned, skinny-yet-muscular, world-affirming prophet from the little crap hole of a village called Nazareth. Nazareth would enjoy further fame with the 1975 release of their greatest hit single, "Hair of the Dog," otherwise known as "the son of a bitch song." Nazareth produced both a Son of God and a son of a bitch. Go figure.

Along with my love and fascination with Jesus has always been a love and fascination with the aforementioned REM. One day I was listening to their song "Talk about the Passion," and decided I would do just that. Michael Stipe sings, "Not everyone can carry the weight of the world" (because he believes Atlas only exists in the glove compartments of our auto vehicles), and this inspired me to attempt to carry the weight of Christology for the entire world. Someone has to do it. If you don't know what Christology is, then read this book. Better yet, google it before you read the book so you won't feel like you walked to school in your underwear.

I am no more qualified to write a book about Jesus than that Muslim guy who pissed off FOX News, and yet I believe with my whole atrial fibrillation-infested heart that Jesus belongs to all of us. Sure, I've got a PhD. Who doesn't? However, I wrote this book not because I'm an expert on religion (although my parents think I am). I wrote this book for every blue-collar, hill-climbing air guitarist who ever woke up one morning and pondered the issue of Jesus' nature and identity. Outside of the realm of science and most of the other subjects we studied in high school (with the exception of study hall), Jesus' question to his disciples "Who do people say I am?" is the most important question we are still asking after all these centuries.

That we are still asking the question means we don't really know what we are talking about. I decided writing one more book about Jesus, which is nothing more than an exercise of urine directional navigation (pissing in the wind), wouldn't hurt anyone. So put your dog outside, grill a chicken breast, tie up your spouse, and tell your kids to work a puzzle. It's time for some serious reading.

Introduction

IN THE SPRING OF 2013 I managed to wrangle a sabbatical out of the congregation I was serving at the time in Louisville, Kentucky, allowing me to spend a few months writing this book. I won't mention the name of the congregation because I'm pretty sure some of the congregants there will not appreciate this book for what it truly is—a splendid work of literary art. I'm not a scholar in the sense of having a business card from an accredited seminary or university, so I approached the writing of this book with the mindset of an artist. Yes, I want the book to be informative, and as accurate as possible, although I don't expect a positive verdict from that group of Christian imitators I like to call "fun-damn-mentalists." I have also included in this book a fair amount of personal information, mainly because I want my children and grandchildren to read the book, call one another and ask, "Did you know that?"

Third, I desired the book to have a humorous, snarky, sarcastic edge to it. I believe this is a rarity in the history of Christian literature. There have been many Christian books written that are funny, although funny in a squeaky clean way. My humor is not necessarily clean or PG-rated, nor is it nasty or R-rated humor just for the sake of being nasty. I have no agenda when it comes to humor. If anyone gets offended by this book it will likely be the theology rather than the humor that ruffles their feathers, though there is a fair amount of humor applied to theology in the book. Maybe theology just makes me laugh more than it does other people.

I may sound a little pretentious when I say this is a book about Jesus for Jesus, but it is. If he can read English then I hope that he will get as much enjoyment out of reading this as I did in writing it. I've often wondered what might be his favorite book about himself—excluding the Gospel of Luke, of course. His favorite rock opera is obviously *Jesus Christ Superstar*, although I'm almost certain he gets sick and tired of seeing tall handsome blue-eyed Euro-Americans playing the role of Jesus. The real Jesus probably looked more like a South American soccer player than a lead singer in a North American rock & roll band.

The order of this book is impeccably orderly, without unnecessary redundancies or contradictions. To use a swimming pool analogy, the reader may sense that I have jumped into the pool of christological thinking without the aid of a diving board, without the proper swimming attire, and yet with a wide variety of swimming techniques at my disposal. The breadth of topics is enough to cause a splash on the nearest sunbather as if I had performed a John Candy cannon ball, while the depth of each topic is shallow enough for those novices who have yet to even perfect the art of flotation in a sea of salt water. I apologize for morphing the analogy from a swimming pool to a sea, although given the fact that water is the common denominator this is excusable. Speaking of salt water, I once "swam" in the Dead Sea in Israel. Before I entered the sea I was convinced that I would be the only person in history who would not float in these waters. I based that conclusion on the fact that no one in the history of humanity was just like me. I have since learned that this was a logical fallacy of some sort. So I learned a very important lesson: I'm not much different than anyone else, with the possible exception of people from Uruguay. I'm pretty sure I don't have much in common with them.

Knowing that I'm very much an average person gave me the justification for penning (or keyboarding) a book about Jesus. I have divided this book into six chapters. Each chapter begins with a number designating which chapter it is, so I hope that clears up any confusion the reader might have, particularly those who think they are reading chapter 1 if they skip over to chapter 3. If this doesn't concern you, just keep reading.

Chapter 1 has all the hallmarks of a writer who sat down at his or her computer one day and decided to start writing aimlessly, sort of what psychologists have us do with "word association." This is a book based on the time-honored method, used mainly in the southern United States and parts of Greenland, of "Jesus association." I simply wrote down everything I could think to write about Jesus, especially if it just came to me in a sudden, unexpected way. This is precisely why this book is a work of art rather than a serious scholarly piece, although you will learn something—guaranteed or your money back. To give you a taste of what's to come in chapter 1, I actually refer to Jesus as a "sinner" and I make the case that the parable of the prodigal son is autobiographical. I tell semi-sappy stories about my family and I try to solve the mystery of human nature. It's all right there in chapter 1. There is no need to read other books about the same topics.

Chapter 2 picks up the pace a bit with the story about how I became a clergyperson. Hint: one of my best friends once told me that becoming a minister was the most radical thing I could do, given who I was. I describe some of the events that led me to become a progressive thinker, even in a West Texas Baptist university. Chapter 2 is the place where you will learn about process theology. I would tell you what process theology entails, but that would spoil the fun of waiting, and I'm pretty sure patience is a virtue in a theological system modeled after the scientific theory of evolution. If this confuses you, then go fishing. You'll see why later. By the way, there is a sex scene in chapter 2 so please hide this book from young readers.

Big Jesus appears on the scene in chapter 3. Originally I wanted to name this chapter (and book) "Big Ass Jesus," but I was afraid the reader would take me too literally. In chapter 3 you will read about Michael Jordan, Napoleon, Elizabeth Kubler-Ross, stray dogs, rodeo clowns, Iris Dement, *Spy vs. Spy*, Anne Rice, David Koresh, near death experiences, atonement theory, Star Wars, Perry the Platypus, the Tasmanian Devil, Paula Dean, the Big Bang theory, the Harlem Globetrotters, Docetism, Viagra, and of course Big Jesus. You can see where I'm going with this, right?

Chapter 4 elevates the discussion with my portrayal of badass Jesus, as articulated in the writings of some of our best historical Jesus scholars. If you are not aware of the Jesus Seminar and you wonder how people could be called "Jesus fellows" with a straight face, then this chapter is for you. I also tell some stories about the badass members of my extended family, most of whom are currently unincarcerated. A fun exercise to do after reading this chapter is to guess what nickname Chris Berman would call you if you played center field for the New York Yankees.

Are you familiar with Emergence Christianity? Me neither. But that's the topic in chapter 5. I do two things in this chapter. First, I talk about Emergence Christianity, and second, I guess what they might have to say about Jesus. It's very scientific. After you read this chapter you will likely get a tattoo, drink more beer and lattes, wear a fashionable retro hat, and grow facial hair, perhaps even if you're a woman, although I'm not real sure about that last point. For certain, however, you will become more generous in your orthodoxy, which I know is on your bucket list.

The final chapter of this book is my very own informed contribution to the history of Christology. I begin by putting the reader in a postmodern hallucination, tell George Zimmerman to stay in his pickup, discuss the "too big to fail" principle as applied to Jesus, criticize C. S. Lewis and Larry Norman, and then launch into my top ten things about Jesus that everyone needs to know before they ever celebrate Christmas again.

And then there's the epilogue, which I have renamed an "Epic Log." If there was any doubt about my creativity and ability to play with words this will surely put those pesky doubts to rest. Oh, and I'm addicted to Diet Cokes. Amen.

--------- 1 ---------

Cut Me Down to Size

In the Gospels, parables are biography; biographies are parables.[1]

A Name Cult

IT'S THE MID-1990S. ONE of my parishioners invites me to sit with her and her family at a church picnic. We are on the front lawn of the little country church near the Mississippi River. A tent provides ample shade from the sun's beams. The grass bends to . . . wait . . . these are way too many details. I'm not a novelist.

Let me start over. Someone in my congregation had the brilliant idea to invite a local "Christian" rock band for the summer picnic's entertainment. Nice young men. They could provide a beat, as my notoriously overactive toe tapping attested. My parishioner seemed pleased, at first, even though she hailed from a pre–baby boomer generation. But after about three songs the lead singer started "praising Jesus." Instantly I looked around hoping to catch a glimpse of this fellow named Jesus because, after all, he provided the lyrics to almost all of their songs. Or was that the Holy Spirit? Either way, human creativity and ingenuity had nothing to do with the production of these songs. It was all God, with Jesus' help, inspired by the Holy Spirit, infused with grace, smothered in faith, ad nauseam.

Still, Jesus was the headliner here. "Praise Jesus!" "Praise the Lord!" "We praise your holy name, Jesus!" "We love you Jesus!" "Jesus gave me

1. I just made that up.

5

the words to this song as I was washing my feet in the bathtub!" Sorry, I just made up that last one, but it might have been said. Then it dawned on me: Jesus is a rock star. "Jesus Christ Superstar," I thought to myself, minus his humanity. I kept these thoughts to myself for a few moments, hiding my embarrassment from the other picnic-goers, hoping their faith was stronger than mine and that all this divine lovemaking wouldn't seem odd to them. While I hoped that my red face could be explained as an unfortunate absence of sunscreen lotion, my parishioner turned to me in total nonchalance and said, "This is a name cult." She nailed it on the head.

Her words continue to ring in my ears to this day. Every time I hear the name Jesus used to solicit an emotional response from an audience the word "cult" comes to mind. Personally speaking, I'm not all that disturbed by the mere presence of cults in our midst. Every religion and pseudo-religion, everything from the corner church to a fraternity to a quilting club, could be construed as a cult. I'm aware that the word "cult" is etymologically related to the word "culture." We all belong to various cults, even if it just entails the habitual watching of *Duck Dynasty* on television. Hell, the American culture that I call the "Consumer Empire" is nothing if not one giant cult. Confession: I have yet to watch a full episode of *Duck Dynasty* because I feel myself being pulled in by a mysterious force. I refuse to drink their Kool-Aid even as I go through each day buying shit I don't need.

This Jesus cult seems to have created an especially large and ubiquitous niche in our culture even as we continue to consume and build an empire. I seriously wonder what Jesus might think about all this. All kidding aside, I think he would throw up, and I thoroughly dislike imagining what divine puke looks like. Or is it divine? Is, or was, Jesus divine? That's a question that might get answered in this book. Or maybe not. Nevertheless, it's one thing to earn a good reputation and occupy a special place in people's hearts. It's quite another thing to get too big for one's britches. But this isn't Jesus' fault. It's ours. We've created a Jesus that is too big. And like the banks in our Consumer Empire, Jesus is "too big to fail."

Why did we put Jesus on such a grand pedestal and why is he still there? Are we afraid that if we knock the legs out from underneath the pedestal the entire thing will crumble? By "the entire thing" I mean the more or less authentic movement Jesus inspired two millennial ago. Perhaps our fears echo the lyrics of Stephen Egerton: "When you cut me down to size I'm like a king that's lost his crown."[2] To state the obvious, Big Jesus isn't

2. Stephen Egerton, "Cut Me Down to Size," from his album *The Seven Degrees of*

going anywhere, at least not anytime soon. No amount of cutting him down to size, no amount of stressing his humanity, no amount of being "honest to Jesus," to quote the late Robert Funk, will take away his crown.[3] Christians around the world will continue to forget that he was once mocked as the "king of the Jews," which would not have occurred even if first-century Palestine held democratic elections. He would have been less popular than a twenty-first-century American Democrat in the Deep South. Christians will continue to pronounce Jesus as the "king of the world," or to use the prophet Isaiah's misquoted words, "Wonderful Counselor, Mighty God, Everlasting Father, Prince of Peace" (9:6). Jesus, don't listen to this! Put your hands over your ears. I don't want you to throw up on my laptop.

What we have created, my dear sisters and brothers in the Christian faith, is a God that is too small in some ways and a Jesus that is too big. Their roles have been reversed. Whereas Jesus intended to point us to God, or more precisely the kingdom of God, now we belong to a cult where most fingers point to Jesus. We worship the finger rather than where the finger was pointing. As we continue to pray to an anthropomorphic (i.e., human-like) deity, we continue to heap praises upon a divinized human being. No offense to Jesus—and none taken, I'm sure—but we need to cut him down to size.

The Sinner

There is a reason Jesus ate with sinners. He was one. By this I don't mean he was a violent drunk, a greasy haired frequenter of Shabbat nightclubs, or someone who burned cats for fun. Jesus was a sinner because "sinner" is nothing more than a code word for flesh-and-blood human animals. In his place and time, being a sinner also meant he hung out with the wrong folks.

As a member of the human race, he had to choose sides. There were not just two sides from which to choose, mind you, although it must have felt as if only two existed. Like many societies, both ancient and contemporary, the gap between those who have a lot and those who have little is

---

Stephen Egerton (2010).

3. Robert Funk founded "The Jesus Seminar" in 1985. They are the scholars who have voted on whether or not the words attributed to Jesus in the four canonical Gospels are authentic or not. I'll share the results of their findings in chapter 4 or 5 or whenever I feel like it. The members of the Jesus Seminar call themselves "Jesus Fellows," which I guess is short for "The Fellowship of Scholars Who Believe Jesus' Divinity Is a Mythological Fairy Tale."

sufficient enough to create social taboos to protect the former (the "haves") from the latter (the "have-nots"). The method of choosing a side, if indeed one had the option of making a choice, was a remarkably simple and symbolic exercise. For a culture lacking in technological distractions such as twitchy dancing fingers on cell phones and food channels on cable television, *eating* was the acceptable method of socialization and, subsequently, social stratification. Who one dined with determined one's place or reputation in a tight-knit, highly networked society that had what we might call a "small town feel."

Jesus ate with sinners because he was one. He was a man with experiences that, for the most part, could be part of almost any man's biography in first-century Palestine, although there was something different about him. The uniqueness of his story was just beginning to take shape when the elites began grumbling about his association with other so-called sinners. Apparently, in their minds he had distinguished himself as someone who had risen above his previously allotted social location among the bottom feeders of society. Now, they believed, was the time to disassociate his self from the vagabonds and sit at table with those who truly deserve his presence. He would never be respected among the elites if he continued to share food with those who likely eat with unwashed hands.

On more than one occasion he didn't hesitate to remind his audience who he was and where he had been. He told his socially mixed audience parables that subtly illustrated his life story, his spiritual journey from isolation to incarnation, from prodigal to provocateur. He once was lost—lost from his roots, his family, his bearings—now he had been found, discovered, returned . . . he had emerged from a place few have ventured. So Jesus peered at his haughty listeners with empathy for their misguided religiosity and at the sinners who stood nearby, daring not to look the elites in the eye, with a sympathetic connection as only a fellow sinner could communicate.

The Gospel writers could not find a way to present his parables of lostness in first-person prose because Jesus was never that interested in removing the mystery from his life and words anyway. Perhaps he liked messing with people's heads—what we in the preaching business call a "mind f___." Well, some of us do anyway. Whatever his motive for mystery, the risk of complete transparency was too high anyway. The Roman Empire's tendency to punish anyone who even hinted that hope could be found among the people of the land was absolute. And yet the autobiographical nature of the parables of lostness is apparent to anyone who can bring the Christ of faith down from the pernicious pedestal his followers created for him after his untimely death. He spoke slowly and succinctly, "Suppose someone among you had one hundred sheep and lost one of them. Wouldn't he leave the other ninety-nine in the pasture and search for the lost one until he finds it?"[4] Although his question was posed in a way that forced an affirmative answer, in reality no one would do such a thing because no shepherd of moderate intelligence would leave his larger flock for one stray. Still, Jesus described the celebratory feeling of finding that one lone lost sheep, the one that got away, the stray . . . the sinner. He was talking about himself.

He remembered, of course, the day he became a man, the day he would learn to stray from the flock. At the age of twelve he traveled with his family to Jerusalem for the festival of Passover. In conversations with the literate temple loiterers he discovered he had acumen for such sacred ponderings. My guess is he found one of those breakfast "wisdom tables" at the local Jerusalem Dairy Queen. No matter where he learned to shine, folks could see that the seeds of sagacity were apparent in him. This incident illuminates the spiritual yearnings that would stay with him the remainder of his life. After several days of conversing, eating, and sleeping in the temple court, his worried parents found him. He was found, and yet ironically he was not yet lost. He already perceived a calling on his life, one that would develop years later after a lengthy period of wandering in the wilderness of discernment—what some, including his family, labeled prodigal or wasteful living.

Later, as a young man, Jesus likely abandoned his family to venture out on his own. We can only speculate where he went and what he did. Did he find a wife and father children? Did he live a nomadic, aimless life? Did he spend time as a disciple of John the Baptizer? Did he go rogue? (Some say he joined Sarah Palin's advisory team, but I believe that's fanciful thinking.) After all, every important religious leader who has ever emerged on the scene began as a rogue, going his or her own way, usually to the point of becoming a problem for the dominant religion of that place and time. Or perhaps the "lost years," as we call them, were spent in ways we have yet to imagine. Don't even try.

We can then surmise that he eventually returned to his family and community in Nazareth, only to be met with rejection if not outright hostility. His first visit to the local synagogue, a story found in Luke 4, in which he personalized the words of the prophet Isaiah, almost resulted in an even more untimely execution than the one that would befall him a few short

4. Luke 15:4 (CEB).

years later. Jesus understood in a personal way the story of his people, the story of exile and return, the story of exodus and homecoming. He lived it. Jesus' parable of the lost sheep, therefore, was not just autobiographical; it was biography for the community. He was speaking on behalf of those who looked downward, those who had never been found, much less celebrated.

He couldn't stop delivering nifty little parables, because the mood was too heavy. Celebration had yet to arrive. The punch line remained elusive. So he continued: "Or what woman, if she owns ten silver coins and loses one of them, won't light a lamp and sweep the house, searching her home carefully until she finds it?"[5] Similar to the parable of the lost sheep, the finder of the coin in this parable would likely use that which is found in order to celebrate the discovery. The sheep likely offers her life for the celebratory meal; the coin is spent on food and wine, tablecloths, and flower arrangements. Discovery leads to celebration; celebration leads to sacrifice. Such is life in the empire and in the shadow of the temple cult. *Celebrate at your own risk, sinner.*

The Prodigal Son

Celebration is risky business, but Jesus knew that being cut off from one's family and community and from one's God is a fate much less desired. After tantalizing his listeners with images of sheep and coins, he decided to get more personal. The following is a reimagining of the parable of the prodigal son. I offer a personalized version of the parable, one that Luke or his future editors were too protective of Jesus' reputation to share, so they offered a version less connected to his life. Imagine Jesus, out of the earshot of his homeys and media handlers, laying down his guard and saying to his listeners:

> My father, Joseph, had several children, including sons that were his pride and joy. As someone who was unsure of my paternal ancestry, I never felt as if I fully belonged. So one day I decided to leave. A few years earlier, I had a taste of separation from my family, discussing matters of God's kingdom with the learned scholars of the temple.[6] My interests and passions were sparked and then slowly nurtured in the womb of Nazareth.

5. Luke 15:8 (CEB).

6. I think Jesus knew early on that using the word "kingdom" in reference to God's realm would really piss off Caesar. It would eventually get him killed. Despite inclusive

Years went by and I needed to get away and discover who I am and what I am about. Borrowing what little I could from my family, I embarked on a soul-searching journey. At first, not understanding the value of the resources I had with me, I lived relatively extravagantly. I wasted everything I had. It did not take long, but by then I was too stubborn to return home and ask to be reinstituted into Joseph's household.

I was hungry, and because of an untimely famine in the land, few people could help me. I was a nomad, living far away from my family, so I took a job with a pig farmer. Pigs and children of Abraham don't really run in the same circles! Unfortunately, the pigs ate better than I did. I had never stooped so low in my life, but it taught me valuable lessons. I knew then where I wanted to be: back in Galilee with my family and friends. I needed a support system, or so I thought. So I began my journey home.

I returned home to the grim news that Joseph had died, and now the household was run by my oldest brother. My family allowed me to dwell in their homes, but I knew that they no longer considered me someone who deserved to be part of this family. And yet, something deep inside of me let me know that I was loved and accepted *regardless*. I didn't know it at the time, but God had already welcomed me with love and compassion. I wanted my family's approval, as anyone would, but I learned that God's acceptance is enough to make me feel as if I'm an honored guest at my own celebratory banquet.

I celebrated my newly discovered identity, however, at my own risk. Celebration of one's place in God's kingdom doesn't sit well with those who live in opposition to God's kingdom. My older brother, in particular, was not amused by my renewed sense of joy and direction. He wasn't feeling it. He continued to accuse me of squandering, wasting my years and resources on everything, including whores. It will take my brother and family more time to accept what I have learned about God. Until then I know just one thing, and I know it deeply, profoundly, and without reservation: *Once upon a time I was lost; but now I am found.*

This is the parable of the prodigal son (Luke 15:11–32) retold as autobiography. Jesus' return to Nazareth to a fatherless household led by his older brothers was likely met with accusations about his years of "wilderness wandering," even of wasteful squandering of resources. The parable that is recorded in Luke's Gospel suggests that the prodigal son's family was

---

language suggestions, I continue to use this word in solidarity with Jesus.

wealthy. Obviously a young man squandering vast resources adds spice to the parable. The amount of squandering, however, is irrelevant. What is relevant is that Jesus' long absence led to the probability of rejection by his family and community. Joseph's son was no longer welcome in Nazareth.

Despite this, his years of spiritual reflection, which may have included his discipleship with John the Baptist and subsequent baptism, and his lengthy journey in a wilderness of temptation, led him to believe that God had brought him into the fold, what he called "the kingdom of God." These experiences compelled him to imagine and proclaim the parables of lostness. They are autobiographical in that they illustrate his life trajectory from lost to found, rejection to acceptance, exile to return. Most interpreters of the parables of lostness conjecture that the primary subjects of authority in these parables (shepherd, woman, father) represent God and God's grace—and they likely do—yet they miss what Jesus was humbly suggesting: that *he* was a sinner like anyone else in need of being discovered, accepted, and celebrated.

When Jesus walked this earth he knew his place. He was not too big for his britches. He was the humble prodigal son, lost as a stray sheep, missing like a coin in the corner of a dark room. He was a man with a story, a profound story that needs to be retold in a way that recreates honest and authentic followers of the finger that pointed to the kingdom of God.

This Is Personal

As a pastor I have seen the theme of lostness played out in the lives of many people. I have sat with families who have lost children in one way or another. I have seen the pain on their faces as they tell me their child has run away from home, has been arrested, or has died by suicide. On more than one occasion I have had to deliver the news to a parent that a son has been killed or have listened to the news that their daughter has been forced to enter into drug rehab. Being a parent is risky business. In the real world not everyone who is lost is found. Like most parents I have an idea what it feels like to lose a child. My tears flow when I watch a scene of parental loss of a child on the small or big screen. Other than my wife's miscarriage, however, I have not experienced the death of a child, and yet the literal and metaphorical theme of lost and found is not totally foreign to me either. The following five stories illustrate with varying degrees of seriousness and heartbreak my personal experiences of lost and found.

When I was a college student in Abilene, Texas in the late 1980s, my family and I lived across the alley from a convenience store. The quickest way to the store was to walk through our backyard gate and around the side of the store to its front door. It was a thirty-second walk at best. One day I told my wife I was going to the store and would be back in a few minutes. For some reason she thought our three-year-old daughter was going with me. I had assumed she wasn't. As I returned home, my wife asked me, "Where's Shanna?" After a brief conversation that let me know I'm not the greatest parent in the world, panic ensued. Our search for her took only a few minutes, but as the old cliché goes, "it seemed like an eternity." She was at the end of the alley crying for her daddy. I think she was just mad she didn't get any candy.

My second story has not always been a happy one, but it's getting there. My son, who spent much of his youth and young adulthood in a prodigal son–like lifestyle, is trying really hard to find his way. A few years ago he entered into a house of meth users, walked into the kitchen to get a drink of water, and became the recipient of a ball of fire hurled in his direction as the makeshift meth lab exploded. Despite his extensive wounds covering a third of his body, the criminal justice system showed little mercy and didn't take too kindly to him hanging out with "tweakers" in a meth lab so he was crowned a Class B felon. This is *his* crown of thorns. His troubles have had a lot to do with an admittedly strained relationship between the two of us. Communication between us has sometimes been scant and forced. At times the relationship is in a state of lostness, but as I look down the road I see someone coming . . .

My third story has a much happier ending. Without going into specific details, in order to protect people's privacy, my wife had to give up a baby for adoption at a very young age for reasons that can't be divulged here. She went on with her life, which included time in a convent, marriage, children, and successful career endeavors, including becoming an advocate for Special Needs children. What she didn't know, or at least suspect, is that the little girl she had given up for adoption wanted to find her. She did. They have reconciled as mother and daughter (with a couple of granddaughters as an added bonus!). Sometimes we don't realize we are lost until someone finds us.

Of course, sometimes the prodigal child—or parent—never returns home. My maternal grandfather left home back in the early 1950s, leaving a wife and *eight* children to fend for themselves. The years went by, my grandmother never remarried, and life was anything but easy for my mother's family. Twenty-five years later we received a phone call from the local police telling us that my grandfather had been found in Arizona. Unfortunately he was deceased. He had been working on a farm in the scorching heat, which proved to be fatal for a man in his sixties. Several of us drove from West Texas to Yuma, Arizona, to identify his body. I was the only grandchild—and there are many of us—to ever see our grandfather in the flesh . . . rotting flesh.

And then there are the grimmest of lost stories. In the early 1900s my paternal great-grandparents lost four young children to meningitis in a span of five days. The five older children, including my grandfather, survived. Not too many years later, at the youthful age of twenty-five, he was sleeping on the passenger side of a truck as it turned a sharp corner. His door came open and he was thrown out into a bundle of barbed wire, bleeding out in a few short hours. My father was still in his mother's womb at the time.

My family understands lost-ness.

An Opportunity

Most Christians are unlikely to agree that the parable of the prodigal son is a critical part of Jesus' own story. They would never believe he was lost in the first place, much less needed to be found. And certainly now Jesus is too big to be lost. Losing Jesus would be like losing a planet in our solar system (unless he is like Pluto, in which case he can just be demoted). Losing Jesus would be unthinkable. The thought that the real Jesus may be missing from the Christian faith, in the sense that we wrongly assume too much about him, is surely seen as heretical and blasphemous. Ironically, as many evangelical Christians place Jesus in their hearts (metaphorically I hope), they have ignored him in their heads. Who he was, what he said and did, and what his life and purpose means for us today reverberates through Christianity like a boxed up wind chime on a breezeless day. In other words, the real Jesus—the lost-then-found prodigal Jesus, the Jesus *before* he was too big for his britches—really *doesn't* reverberate at all in the wooden pews on Sunday mornings. Too few preachers and priests talk about this Jesus.

Therefore, we are missing a really big opportunity to connect with folks. Many people recognize the lost-to-found trajectory in their own lives or in their family history in various ways and to various degrees. The parables of lostness speak to them in profoundly personal ways. We, however, have created a Jesus that is too big to connect with us in profoundly personal ways. We have unnecessarily stripped him of his proverbial hobo knapsack, like the Roman soldiers stripped him of his garments. We have robbed him of his humanity.

Are we comfortable with the savior on a cross, taking on the sins of the world like Atlas holding the entire world on his shoulders, or can we see the cross for what it is: the tragic end of a man who had much more wisdom to share with us? Can we learn to see the crown of thorns on his head as just that—a source of pain and bloodshed—rather than a symbol of the crown of a king who secretly rules the universe? Have we missed opportunities to lift up the real Jesus, not on a mystical cross or a misguided pedestal, but as a man who had real needs and real things to say to real people?

The key to understanding Jesus, in my mind, is to look at the parables as largely autobiographical rather than as Zen-like anecdotes meant to stupefy the stupid, leaving burgeoning Christian rock stars scrambling for the right words of praise. We have created a religion where the most profound utterance is "Praise Jesus!" because we have stripped him down to his name and nothing else.

Jesus' parables of lostness are real—real words for real folks. They are not just biographical, however, for those individuals who have experienced rejection in family and community or even with God. They are also biographical for the church as a whole, the community spawned by the early Jesus movement that continues to live, change, and emerge from the shadow of the too-big-to-fail Jesus in the twenty-first century. If nothing else, the church is the body of Christ in the world today and therefore the prodigal child par excellence.

The church has wasted and squandered centuries of creative spiritual and intellectual energy on theological exercises of futility, primarily about Jesus. We have flirted, indeed whored, with a high Christology that is only relevant for those who feel compelled to understand Jesus as some kind of divinely chosen solution to a problem of our own limited imagination: sin. As an answer to this contrived problem Jesus has proved to be insufficient and unsatisfactory for many. After all, we are *still* sinning, and we still feel guilty on occasion, and we still ask for forgiveness. When is this damn formula of salvation going to start working? Our problem is that we experience this "savior" as a square peg in a round hole. If we are honest with ourselves nothing quite fits and yet we continue along this path for fear of further rejection and ostracism from both God and the community of faith.

Jesus has been lost to us and now he is returning—or rather emerging—at this moment in history. This is our moment, our opportunity to move beyond pious rhetoric toward something more authentic. This is an exciting time to be people who desperately need Jesus to be relevant, coherent, and palatable. To call this a "second coming" is both arbitrary (this could be a third, fourth, fifth, etc. "coming") and confusing to those who are looking for a corporeal appearance on something like a fire-breathing horse. (Personally, I wish someone would update second coming scenarios so that Jesus is depicted as coming back in a spaceship. Oh wait, the Heaven's Gate cult already did something like that and they ended up drinking the Kool-Aid! Never mind. Stick with the horses or clouds or whatever the apocalyptic writers imagined while they were hiding from the Romans and smoking something they shouldn't have been smoking.)

Something tangible is now stirring in the caldron of Christian thought. I will likely be burned at the stake for witchcraft for using the word "caldron," so I should retract that statement. Nevertheless, allow me to continue: The thesis of this book is that Jesus has been lost, but now is on the verge of being found. The real Jesus—the flesh-and-blood Jesus—was rejected, but now there is a promise of acceptance. Jesus, the man from Nazareth, was in exile but now, knapsack in hand, is emerging from the forest. He has come to his senses and so are we. We should embrace and celebrate even if celebration is risky business.

The News

Because I am so adamant that Jesus should be viewed first and foremost as a human being mired in the human condition, I should say a word about the human condition. Better yet, I should share what I believe Jesus, my sponsor, would say about the human condition. By calling Jesus my "sponsor" I'm not suggesting that he is bankrolling the publication of this book. That would be silly because Judas probably pocketed all of his money. Jesus is my sponsor much like an alcoholic procures a sponsor from his/her local AA group. In other words, I suffer from humanity, and Jesus, a fellow human being who had/has his shit figured out better than I do, is my sponsor. Or at least I like to think so.

Anyway, what did Jesus think about the human condition? Just asking that question reminds me of a colleague I knew years ago. I followed him in the pulpit at a particular unnamed congregation. He retired there, continued to worship there, and had a very intimate relationship with his wristwatch, which he kept staring at while I preached each and every Sunday morning. (Can you tell I'm still irked?) This reverend told me he loved to tell his congregation that "the problem with the church is people . . . and the problem with people is they are no damn good." This is the kind of wisdom I absorbed over the years.

But are we really "no damn good"? I believe we certainly think we are. Perhaps we invented "the News" (in newspapers, on the radio, television, Internet, etc.) so we could wake up every morning and remind ourselves how utterly rotten, depraved, wicked, evil, and immoral humanity really is. What I love (or not) about the News is how it has a knack for pointing to the obvious examples of human depravity. It gives us the impression that human evil is ubiquitous, like a green slime that will sooner or later seep through the walls of our homes and hearts. Examples of the imperfect human condition abound: war, terrorism, murder, physical and sexual abuse, oppression, discrimination, drug trafficking, sex slaves, theft, arson . . . the Tea Party. One of my favorite human depravity stories of all time is about a man wearing a Texas Longhorns t-shirt who walked into a bar in Oklahoma and was severely injured by an Oklahoma Sooners fan. What does homicidal rage over one's favorite college football team say about the human condition?

I realize most people do not consider themselves capable of doing such things. Most of us are not serial killers, do not destroy cats in microwave ovens, and are not prone to fly off in a fit of homicidal rage over a football or soccer game. (Although I'm not so sure about soccer fans . . . May I rant for a moment? Why the hell are so many people enamored with soccer? I realize that most, if not all, really good soccer players are excellent athletes, but why are they wasting time on a game played *without hands*? Shouldn't we reserve this game for people who suck at hand-eye coordination? Isn't this a social justice issue?) Still, if we think our lives are completely guilt free or that we have somehow evolved beyond any hint of animalistic depravity (defined here as our obsession to eat, have sex, and kill things) then we are sadly mistaken. Perhaps we have allowed our memories to take a senility vacation. My old colleague may have been right: We *are* no damn good!

The biblical writers, almost without exception, had a very similar understanding of the human condition. The prophet Jeremiah, a highly efficient and yet grossly underpaid spokesperson for the Creator of the universe, said (using the Creator's "scary voice"), "For my people are foolish, they do not know me; they are stupid children, they have no understanding. They are skilled in doing evil, but do not know how to do good."[7] Wow. Not only are the people evil; they are *skilled* in doing evil. To be skilled at something usually takes practice. I suggest that when we see blatant examples of evil in the News it is often a practiced skill. Before the murderer, rapist, or abuser gets caught he or she has probably already put in a lot of good practice time. Malcolm Gladwell argues in his book *Outliers: The Story of Success* that to be proficient at something we need to spend about ten thousands hours in practice.[8] Just so you know, I'm very good at eating and sleeping. I'm also very good at walking, holding my head up, and peeing.

The writer of Psalm 14 had a similar pessimistic view of the human condition: "Fools say in their hearts, there is no God. They are corrupt and do evil things; not one of them does anything good. The Lord looks down from heaven on humans to see if anyone is wise, to see if anyone seeks God, but all of them have turned bad. Everyone is corrupt. No one does good— not even one person."[9] I love the translation that says, "They do abominable deeds," which implies that snowmen are evil. But I digress. Although Psalm 14 has a somewhat happy ending for the good guys (the Israelites), the bad guys (pretty much everyone else) are gonna get it. Even if they start out as "good," perhaps as babies, they will eventually turn bad like the high-school-chemistry-teacher-turned-meth-maker on the hit television show *Breaking Bad*. We are, to use the acronym for my intramural college basketball team, "SOTE" (Scum Of The Earth), and we all deserve to die a horrible, excruciating, nails-torn-from-the-fingers-and-toes death.

This may be why some people are uncomfortable reading the Hebrew Scriptures (the Old Testament). This ancient collection of books begins with a couple who wins Eddie Money's "Two Tickets to Paradise," Adam and Eve, and who messes things up (for all people apparently) by eating from a tree that was supposed to be off limits. Who can blame them? I mean, who wouldn't want to eat from a tree with tasty fruit that makes one smarter and wiser! As the story goes, however, this pissed off God. God is like, "Oh no you did-n't!" After that, Adam has to grow his own fruit,

7. Jeremiah 4:22 (NRSV)

8. Gladwell, *Outliers*, 35–68.

9. Psalm 14:1–2 (CEB).

Eve has to go through labor pains, and the snake has to, well, do what all snakes do and crawl on its belly . . . which is not a big deal because snakes don't have any legs anyway. By the way, I'll let the reader know what *really* occurred in the garden of Eden in the next chapter. I write this provocative statement so you'll keep reading.

Some early Christian theologians such as Irenaeus, Tertullian, Cyprian, Ambrose, Ambrosiaster, and Augustine looked at this mythological account of human origins and other passages in the Old and New Testaments and decided that Adam's sin is passed on from one generation to the next. Those guys had a better imagination than I do! The doctrine of original sin, as it is called, suggests that human nature is sinful, evil, guilty, or even depraved (to various degrees, depending on who you ask). The "problem" of original sin has proven to be very lucrative for the church because it ostensibly offers the "answer" to the problem of sin . . . something about Jesus dying on the cross, which I will poo-poo later. (I won't poo-poo the dying part, just the "answer" part.) "Outside the church there is no salvation," said Cyprian of Carthage, a third-century bishop. The church has been making money ever since. After all, it has a corner on the salvation market.

Whether the doctrine of original sin is true or not—and I suspect it is horse crap of the smelliest order—the primary witness of Scripture and church is that human beings are about as trustworthy as a puppy dog with an old leather shoe. And we shall suffer for that, sayeth the Lord. The Old Testament ends with Malachi, who also manages to quote the Lord in the Lord's scary voice, saying, "See, the day is coming, burning like an oven, when all the arrogant and all evildoers will be stubble."[10] God affirms that the "righteous" will be okay, but anyone who reads this has got to at least consider the possibility that he or she may be more of an "evildoer" than not. I know I do. I cannot go into details, but the worst thing I ever did in my entire life involved an ice machine in the Texas panhandle. Don't ask. All I know is I'm in big trouble if God decides to show a digital recording of my life to his top angel officials.

So, by all accounts, both ancient and contemporary, the human condition is noted for a few rough edges. The Old Testament's pessimistic view of humanity simply confirms what we read or hear in the News every day: that we are no damn good . . . which is why Christians have a hard time viewing Jesus as a human being. If he's human then he's no damn good and that would suck for us.

10. Malachi 4:1a (NRSV).

The Better Angels of Our Nature

Fortunately, there are other witnesses to the human condition that tell a different story. These witnesses tell us that, yes, the human condition leaves a lot to be desired; after all, we are nothing more (or less) than animals with bigger than average brains. However, it may not be as bad as it looks. The more astute observers of evil in the world recognize that the News is more exception than rule. Steven Pinker, in his book, *The Better Angels of Our Nature: Why Violence Has Declined*, laboriously and convincingly makes the case that we are living in the least violent era in human history. This is the premise of his entire book; however, I only read about the first 250 pages and then decided I would ironically die a violent death at the hands of my wife if I continued to ignore her by spending all my free time reading the book. Pinker suggests we are evolving and becoming more humanitarian and civilized. His view differs from the Old Testament perspective in that he argues humanity *comes out of* a previously more animalistic, violent genetic pool, whereas the Old Testament suggests we began in a state of pristine goodness, then screwed up royally. This became evident when Coca-Cola Bottling Company tried to replace Classic Coke with New Coke. Whoever came up with that idea is likely going to hell.

The Greek philosopher Aristotle echoed the Old Testament perspective, yet only to a certain point. He believed that human beings are by nature good and virtuous. And this from a man who taught Alexander the Great, one of the most maniacal warmongers of all time! Aristotle argued that humans begin with a capacity for goodness, which has to be developed and nurtured by practice. Just as we can be skilled in doing evil, as Jeremiah suggests, we can also become skilled in doing good.

The difference between Aristotle and the New Testament is that the former believed we have the capacity to transcend or move beyond our own moral weaknesses. The latter, however, suggests we need "a little help from Above." The Apostle Paul's story is a case in point. He tells his protégé, Timothy, that he was "formerly a blasphemer, a persecutor, and a man of violence." He calls himself the "foremost" of sinners, which means he must have had a lot of practice! Then he was knocked off his high horse (if indeed he was riding a horse) on the road to Damascus. After a brief time of blindness Paul finally "saw the light" and became a follower of Jesus. He tells Timothy that Jesus strengthened him and judged him to be faithful, appointing him to Jesus' service. He also claims he received mercy and grace and had become "an example to those who would come to believe in him

(Jesus) for eternal life."[11] By his own admission, Paul was mired in the mud of the human condition and was pulled out of that mud by Jesus the Christ. He got a little help from above.

So which is it? Did humanity begin in a pristine state of goodness, only to "break bad" and share our evil nature with our offspring? Or did we begin, and do we continue to be, in a state of Tennyson's "Nature: red in tooth and claw"? Regardless of how we began, where are we now? Do we have an innate capacity for goodness, or are we hardwired for mischief, or is humanity a fascinating swirl of inclinations we have labeled "good" and "bad"?

And where is Jesus on all this? Well, of course, not to tip my hand and revel in my biases, but I believe Jesus was somewhat of a master on the human condition because, again, *he was one.* He knew humanity's temptations, weaknesses, and erring ways. He also seems to have been much more optimistic about us than most of his contemporaries. Going back to the fifteenth chapter of Luke's Gospel we find Jesus once again eating with those who were considered to be the most susceptible to the whims of human evil: "tax collectors and sinners." Why are tax collectors and sinners separated here? "Sinners" refers to the general state of just about everyone who wasn't part of the "in crowd" in that day, but tax collectors were so bad, so evil, that they transcended or exceeded the normal parameters of sinfulness! They needed their own special category of sinfulness.

Jesus willingly ate side by side with these despicable people, angering the religious elites. So he used his "teacher voice" (as opposed to the "scary voice" of the earlier prophets) and shared his parables of lostness with folks who, according to conventional wisdom, were either lost (the sinners) or found (the elites). These parables border on absurdity and yet they tell us a lot about Jesus' understanding of the human condition. Here we have a vision of humanity that is *inherently good but* . . . and that's a mighty big but. We are not born in sin as the doctrine of original sin suggests. We are born in goodness (or perhaps neutrality, a "blank slate") *but* for various reasons we often lose our way. We become lost, we are found, and then lost, found, lost . . . it ain't black and white. Most of us identify with this grayish assessment of humanity.

Regardless of whether the gray is closer to black or white, I will put on my clergy hat for a moment and give everyone a huge cosmic hug by saying this: According to Jesus, who struggled with his own feelings of lostness,

11. 1 Timothy 1:12–16 (NRSV).

God finds us, affirms us, loves us, and sends us on our way to discover the good in others. This is the human condition. I hope that doesn't make us too big for *our* britches.

2

Part One of a Bewildered Semi-Conscious Meandering Autobiography

When [I was asked] to write a spiritual autobiography, my first impulse was to decline. That was also my second impulse, and my third. For I have at least three good reasons not to do such a thing. First, I have already written something called an "Intellectual Autobiography"; the rule At most one to a customer *seems to me an excellent one for autobiographies; more than one is unseemly. Second, my spiritual life and its history isn't striking or of general interest: no dramatic conversions, no spiritual heroism, no internal life of great depth and power; not much spiritual sophistication or subtlety, little grasp of the various depths and nuances and shading and peculiar unexplored corners of the spiritual life: very much an ordinary meat and potatoes kind of life. (It is also, I regret to say, a life that hasn't progressed nearly as much as, by my age and given my opportunities, it should have.) Third, writing any kind of autobiography has its perils; but writing a spiritual autobiography is particularly perilous. The main problem has to do with truthfulness and honesty: there are powerful temptations toward self-deception and hypocrisy . . . Truth in our innermost being is not easy to achieve. It is hard to see what the truth is; it is also hard to tell the truth, to say what you see without imposing some kind of self-justificatory and distorting framework.*[1]

1. Alvin Plantinga, "Spiritual Autobiography."

23

The Customer Is Always Right

If Alvin Plantinga can admit to not having progressed in life as far as he should have when he wrote those words, then I feel like a ten-speed bike stuck in first gear. As Jeanne Robertson relates in her comic standup routine about her husband, I am "over-degreed."[2] Somehow I managed to attain a PhD from Baylor University in 1996 writing a dissertation on war and peace at exactly the same time a television commercial was airing about someone writing a dissertation on war and peace. For the life of me I can't remember what that commercial was about, probably because its product didn't concern a financially struggling minister with three small children. I do remember my dissertation, however. It is titled *The Emerging Concept of Just Peace Theory*. You can't buy it on amazon.com. I guess that means that dissertations on war and peace are a dime a dozen, but frankly I don't care. (This lack-of-care attitude, which I proudly introduce with the word "whatever" as much as I can, is exactly why I haven't progressed in my career as quickly as I would have liked.) Now that I have reached such an advanced age, however, it might be helpful to rehash my spiritual journey in order to determine why today I think *Jesus is too big*.

I haven't been to a therapist for this, but I believe a properly degreed therapist might trace the roots of my low Christology (which I will define later) to a mom-and-pop grocery store in a small town in West Texas. (I'm fairly certain no one has ever said that before!) If the knowledge I derived from a college Intro to Psych course is correct, much of who we are and what we think and do can be traced back to our childhoods. My particularly unenchanted childhood was spent bagging groceries, stocking shelves, and grinding hamburger meat in my parents' little drive-in grocery store. I learned some valuable lessons working in that store. First, I learned that two people—mainly my folks—can each work half a day and still make a decent living, especially with the cheap labor my siblings and I provided over the years. (If you loan my parents a copy of this book, please tear out this page.) Second, I learned that whistling while one works gives the impression that one is happy. Thanks for that, Dad. Third, and most importantly, I learned that *the customer is always right*. One should never argue with a customer about anything unless they are obviously wrong. For example, I had to agree with a cattle rancher that eating steak on Thanksgiving is the right and proper thing to do.

2. See her website, http://www.jeannerobertson.com/.

So what does the timeless truth that "the customer is always right" have to do with my spiritual roots? I've thought about this—I really have—more than I care to admit. It's probably the reason why, years later, I studied ethics at Baylor University and wrote a dissertation on war and peace. I had an abiding urge (whatever that means) to know the difference between right and wrong, good and evil, just and unjust, etc. Ethically speaking, *is* the customer always right? Of course not, but what my parents instinctively knew ("instinctively" because they didn't study ethics in college like I did) is that the issue is not about the customer's rightness or wrongness; the issue is about the decisions and behaviors of the store clerks or owners. Money, of course, was a motivating factor for my folks' ethical principle of the always-correct customer, even when money was lost in a particular transaction. However, giving preference to the perspective of the customer was almost always the right thing to do, especially in a small town! It pays off in the long run.

The principle "the customer is always right" affected me spiritually in another, less obvious way. I will explain: The culture in which I was raised was and is Baptist in the sense that no matter what church one attends in West Texas, or the Deep South for that matter, there is a distinct evangelical if not fundamentalist flavor to the theological viewpoints of many people. Some people refer to this as the "Bible Belt." The belt is awfully wide in this country! Even if one visits a Methodist, Presbyterian, or other mainline Protestant church on a Sunday morning in the South, the sermons, hymns, and prayers will sound remarkably similar.

Sometimes the sermons at the same church will sound remarkably similar from week to week. While enrolled at Hardin-Simmons University in the mid-1980s I was invited to attend a fellow student's rural Baptist church. Although he was only an undergraduate student, he pastored that congregation. He wanted me to teach a Sunday school class, probably because he noticed something special about me. Or not. I attended three Sundays in succession. My friend preached the very same sermon each time: same theme with different illustrations. His sermons had something to do with trying to get each and every poor sinner in the audience to repent and believe in Jesus Christ as their personal savior. I was confused. Did I need to "repent" or could I just "believe"? I often wish evangelicals would make up their minds.

Before I left my parents' business to go to college, the doctrine of "inerrancy" was gaining a lot of steam in evangelical Christianity. Although I wasn't much interested in religion until my early twenties, I couldn't help but absorb the always implied and sometimes yelled view that *the Bible is always right* . . . even more right than the customers in my parents' grocery store. Inerrancy, by the way, means "without error." Proponents of biblical inerrancy claim to believe that every word in the Bible—usually the King James Version—is theologically, ethically, historically, and scientifically accurate in every way. Frankly, I'm appalled that God needed six days to create the world.

The Discovery of Acumen

My memory of those years isn't the best, and yet I probably believed in an inerrant ("the Bible is always right") Bible without giving much thought to the subject. I was a college dropout, working in my parents' grocery store, and married with a couple of little girls. Even if I did believe wholeheartedly in an error-free Bible, I seemed to have thought everyone else's understanding of the Bible was skewed. I had given up the habitual use of marijuana in those days and substituted it for an addiction to religion— the kind where people speak in tongues, the minister doesn't prepare a sermon, and if you *don't* raise your hands in praise to Big Jesus everyone stares at you. It was at this point in my life that I learned a very important thing about myself: If everyone else does or thinks one thing, I'm damned sure going to think and do something different. Every Bible study in that little Assemblies of God church I was attending in those days ended with my protestations about everyone else's interpretation of Scripture, creating a lot of discomfort in those sincere theologically naïve souls that met on Wednesday evenings in a former Woodmen of the World community building. It is fair to assume that I was also a theologically naïve soul at that time. Some would say I still am.

Let me return to the amateur psychology I have already exhibited in this chapter. The reason I may have been so argumentative in Bible study, the reason why I always felt the need to wander off in a different theological direction, is probably due to the fact that I spent my entire childhood as a proverbial fish out of water. My social location should not have been my social location. Moving from a mid-sized city to a small rural community at the age of ten will do that to you. I arrived at my little elementary school in Sterling City, Texas, in January of 1970, wearing striped bell-bottoms and a black turtleneck sweater. My male classmates, I would soon learn as I walked past an overweight Mexican-American janitor named "Pancho" who eyed me with amusement and suspicion, were all wearing cowboy hats, blue jeans, belt buckles that covered their entire bellies, and cowboy boots. I also seem to remember that they were dipping snuff in class—although I'm sure my memory of fourth grade is a little off kilter these days. My point is that I grew up exhibiting oppositional behavior, seemingly out of necessity, as much as I could without getting the shit kicked out of me. I'm not sure if this is why members of the subculture of West Texas are called "shitkickers," but it fit in nicely with the nickname with which I tagged everyone who asked a stupid question ("No shit, Sherlock!"), and also in anticipation that someday I would be a Dr. Watson. This was just one of those nice little coincidences in life.

Fast forward to my early twenties: After a couple of years with the tongue-talkers, I met the new Baptist preacher in town, a young man recently graduated from Golden Gate Baptist Theological Seminary. Imagine a Texan going to seminary in San Francisco and coming back to Texas to pastor a Baptist church in a town with a population less than a thousand souls and the only town in the entire county, a county that was populated with cattle and sheep ranches and shitkickers. If you can imagine that person then you know Bob Webb. He was one of those "moderates": highly intelligent and, like me, very much a fish out of water in that small West Texas town. He came by our grocery store most mornings for a Dr. Pepper, the breakfast of choice for many people in that land of paradise. One day he invited me to his church's "January Bible study," an annual event where a professor from a neighboring Baptist university or seminary visits a Baptist church and leads the flock in old-fashioned Bible study. I decided to go because I figured a tongue-talking Pentecostal like me knew a lot more about the Bible than a Baptist professor. I was wrong. However, one night the professor invited me over to the Baptist preacher's parsonage, sat me down, and told me I had "acumen" for religious studies.

Although I didn't know what that word meant, the chance encounter certainly changed my life. He invited me to attend his university, Hardin-Simmons. He told me that if I attended I would be "one of the most educated people in the world." Obviously. So, later that week I sat my parents down and told them I would no longer be available to watch their store so they could fly to Vegas and spend my inheritance. A few months later, much like the Beverly Hillbillies without the Texas Tea, I loaded up my family and traveled off to the big Baptist university *a hundred miles away.* All I knew is that I had plenty of gas in the tank and Big Jesus in my heart. Better not mess with this dude or he'll kick the shit out of you . . .

27

Peeling the Onion

Even before I arrived on campus, my relatively uninformed social, political, and religious leanings had moved decidedly to the left. Most of that can be attributed to the young Baptist minister who, along with the January Bible study professor, Dr. James Shields, encouraged me to go back to college. The politics of West Texas were changing from yellow dog Democratic dominance to the "It's morning in America" feel-good conservatism of the Reagan years, but my preacher friend would stand in the pulpit and, if memory serves me correctly, pronounce that he was a Democrat. The county chairperson of the Republican Party was a member of that congregation. I remember her politely disagreeing with him, and yet there was mutual respect between them. Obviously that wouldn't happen today! I voted for Reagan against Carter in 1980, but in the ensuing politically charged years of a Republican White House, a final fundamentalist takeover of the Southern Baptist Convention, and the subsequent "marriage" between evangelical Christianity and the Republican Party, I would never vote for another Republican or knowingly share a chocolate milkshake with a fundamentalist, a member of the Moral Majority, or a Pat Robertson Christian Broadcasting Network addict again. Sorry to sound so dated.

Another important factor in my move to the left, religiously speaking, was a book my then-mother-in-law gave to me as a gesture of goodwill as I readied myself for religious studies in college. That book was Thomas Sheehan's *The First Coming*. I seriously doubt my conservative mother-in-law previewed the book before she gave it to me. She probably assumed it would also explain Christ's *second* coming with the necessary charts and timetables for Jesus' return to planet Earth. Nevertheless, I will never forget how this book opened my mind to the possibility that much of what we assume we know about Jesus *just isn't so*. Sheehan may not have used charts to outline the Parousia, but he produced a chart outlining *how Jesus became God* (which is just a fancy way of referring to Big Jesus). If you are unsure of the definition of the word "Parousia," look it *up* (pun intended).

Sheehan argues that if we read the New Testament chronologically we will see clear evidence of an evolution of christological thinking. The evolution looks like this:

- Jesus becomes the Son of Man at his second coming (Simon Peter; c. 30 C.E.).

- Jesus is exalted as Lord at his resurrection (Paul; 50 C.E.).

- Jesus is adopted as Christ at his baptism (Mark; 70 C.E.).

- Jesus is begotten as savior at conception (Matthew/Luke; 85 C.E.).

- Jesus becomes God-man at incarnation and is eternally God before creation (Colossians hymn; John; c. 50–100 C.E.)[3]

Notice how Jesus' acquisition of divinity keeps moving to an earlier event as the writings of the New Testament progress chronologically. As my great-grandmother used to say as she spit her nasty chaw tobacco into her spittoon and thread a panicky worm onto her hook, "There's something fishy going on." (My great-grandmother also loved to shell pecans. Fishing for catfish on the river bottoms and shelling pecans are both hobbies one can do while accurately spitting chaw tobacco.) That whole inerrancy thing was about to lose its next devotee. Largely due to my reading of Sheehan's book, when I arrived on campus at Hardin-Simmons in Abilene, Texas, in the fall of 1985, I was as prepared as one could possibly be in my theologically embryonic state to have my Sunday school faith and theology shaken to the core.

Others were not so prepared. The first class I took at Hardin-Simmons was titled, "Methods of Biblical Interpretation." One of the first biblical theologians introduced to the class by Dr. George Knight was the twentieth-century German scholar Rudolf Bultmann. Bultmann helped us understand *why* there seems to be an evolution in the New Testament's Christology, generally speaking from "low" to "high." For the purposes of this book, "low" Christology emphasizes Jesus' humanity whereas "high" Christology elevates Jesus in his divinity. (High Christology has nothing to do with marijuana, even in Colorado.) As a form critic, Bultmann and others understood that the various "pericopes" or units of material in the Gospels reflect the theological testimony of the various communities that produced them. Form criticism cannot get us back to the "Jesus of history" but it can inform us how the "Christ of faith" developed during the subsequent decades after Jesus' death. Bultmann did not believe Jesus made any grandiose claims about himself. Jesus would not have considered himself to be "messianic" or "divine." Those sentiments would develop later within the early community of Jesus' followers.

Bultmann viewed the high Christology and many of the other more incredulous claims of the New Testament as unsustainable teachings for people in the twentieth century. He still thought there is a compelling message in the New Testament—what he called the "kerygma" (proclamation

---

3. Sheehan, *First Coming*, 194.

of the Gospel)—but in order to understand the kerygma we must wade through the mythological worldview and terminology of the New Testament. We must peel back the multiple layers of mythology in the Gospels as one peels an onion. Some of the mythology Bultmann rejected includes the biblical view of a three-story world (heaven, earth, and hell), miracles, eschatological (end of times) expectations, sacrificial atonement, the resuscitation of a corpse (resurrection), etc. Bultmann called the onion peeling process on the Gospels "demythologization," which is as fun to pronounce as it is to use as a conversation starter on the golf course. I'm serious; no one can make a putt after hearing that word.

As I said, others were not as prepared as I was to ignite a theological bomb in their heads and let the pieces fall where they may. The concept of demythologization made a couple of young wannabe preacher boys cry—after all, we were talking about peeling back an onion! They left school and, unless they enrolled somewhere in a Bible college where Rudolf Bultmann's name was never uttered, they probably took up careers in paintbrush design or lip-reading couples in restaurants. What is funny to me is that Bultmann is not even considered to be a *liberal*, relatively speaking, in the world of biblical scholarship.

Who? Me? A Feminist?

Looking back, my years at Hardin-Simmons University, a Southern Baptist school with religion professors of the more moderate variety, were very fruitful in the *deconstruction* of the Sunday school faith of my childhood and the Pentecostal/charismatic experiences of my early twenties. I learned a lot in those days, most of it long forgotten. It's more like I just absorbed it all into my skin like a tattoo . . . and it ain't coming out. I have to be careful, as my January Bible study professor and subsequent teacher of theology, Dr. Shields, told me on more than one occasion, "Brother Jimmy, you will never be able to share eighty percent of what you have learned at this school from a Baptist pulpit." Fortunately, after I left Hardin-Simmons in 1989 I would never preach from a Baptist pulpit again. And yes, I do use much of what I have learned in school in my sermons. I mean, if a goat roper from West Texas can handle it without having a nervous breakdown, so can others. By the way, a goat roper is distinguished from a shitkicker in that the former is a wannabe cowboy who wears his jeans inside his boots. A real cowboy (or shitkicker) knows that if you do that you will end up with a substantial amount of cow shit in your boots.

Dr. Shields is responsible for a lot of the freedom I have experienced in my meandering spiritual journey. With his crew cut hairstyle and bull-doggish looks, he resembled Gomer Pyle's sergeant. His teaching style was almost militaristic. He read word for word from his notes, expecting us to write down precisely every single syllable. There was *no* discussion until a few minutes before class was due to expire. At that point he would allow us to comment on the day's topic, which would often delve into a spirited debate. I will never forget how he would bring an end to the class by pound-ing his hand on his desk and saying authoritatively, "Boys, thank God we're saved by grace and not by doctrine!" The only disappointing thing about this, aside from the notion that we need to be "saved," is that he rarely said it to any girls because, well, Baptist girls apparently have cooties and are unlikely to study theology.

My universe was still not quite so large that I couldn't ask myself where and how I fit into the general scheme of things. Who was I? If I should find a place in this convoluted institution called the church, if I should find a place in the realm of God, where would my chair be located? A spiritual journey is, if nothing else, a search for one's identity. Without realizing it, I was a prodigal son of West Texas, wandering further and further away from the values of a shitkicker worldview. To say I was "lost" was a gross "mis-underestimation" of just how far a person can journey from their culturally assigned roots. (God bless George W. Bush for that word.)

One day, immediately following a class that *did* pertain to members of the female gender, I was sitting in an eatery on the campus of Hardin-Simmons when a young lady approached me in a state of mischievousness mixed with shyness. She said, "Excuse me, may I ask you a question?" I was startled. Women were rarely so forward with me. I said, "You may." She then asked, "Are you a feminist?" Of course, I wasn't all that familiar with the word, but I probably had a working knowledge of its meaning. I answered, "Can a guy be a feminist?" She said "Yes, of course," to which I replied, "Well, then, I guess I'm a feminist." She then proceeded to tell me that there were certain things I had said in class that made her think I had feminist sensitivities. (I have since discovered that my personality is rather androgynous, which has nothing to do with the fact that I can play ping-pong equally well with both hands.) My self-perception was beginning to come into focus, which is not unusual for someone in his mid-to-late twen-ties. The prodigal son was perhaps never going to return to West Texas—at least not philosophically—but I was also beginning to realize the value of a non-pigeonholed identity.

Another word that wouldn't show up on my radar for a while was "postmodern." Without even knowing what the word meant, I was entering into what some call a postmodern world. The fragile sticks I had used in my life that served as a foundation for my religious beliefs had snapped, and my spiritual wilderness wandering would have to wait before I would ever reach a meaningful level of *reconstruction*. I was now "lost" in the sense that a tent revivalist would probably not understand, and yet my theological, sociological, and political world had opened up like the big West Texas sky I would soon leave behind.

Is Your Name Really Dr. Christian?

After I received my bachelor's degree from Hardin-Simmons I was encouraged to stay put and pursue a master's degree in religion rather than go to seminary. I did this thinking that I would eventually move back home, manage my folks' grocery store, and become a glorified Sunday school teacher at the local Baptist church. Pursuing a master's was a great experience. For this degree I focused on Old Testament studies under the tutelage of Dr. Donnie Auvenshine. (A preferable label is "Hebrew Scriptures" but I don't want to lose the reader at such an early stage in the reading of this masterpiece of non-fiction literature.) Dr. Auvenshine was new to Hardin-Simmons and the teaching profession and was looking for a few recruits to take his classes. Because I am a "rescuer" (according to my friends) I obliged and spent the next couple of years taking courses in Old Testament studies. Dr. Auvenshine and I would become even closer when we traveled with a group to Israel in the summer of 1988 for a "dig," known among more professional writers as an "archaeological excavation." The reason we became closer is because we were assigned the same "square," which is archaeology-speak for a designated spot to shovel dirt and look for ancient artifacts. You really get to know a person by spending five weeks together in a square "accidentally" throwing dirt on one another.

The most significant day spent in northern Israel, however, was the day Dr. Auvenshine and I both acquired a mean case of diarrhea, probably due to drinking the water. "Don't drink the water" in a foreign country, I learned the hard way, is not something that needs to be demythologized. It's just true. We stayed in our youth hostel all day long talking about life and plans for the future as we developed a rotating schedule on the toilet.

I told him I didn't think I could be a Baptist preacher and that I had read a lot about the United Church of Christ and found it more "edgy." He agreed and said I should pursue ministry in the UCC. Therefore, when people ask me what inspired me to become a United Church of Christ clergyperson I always tell them that an Old Testament professor with the "runs" in a youth hostel in northern Israel told me I would suck as a Baptist preacher. (As an aside, my trip to Israel inspired my master's thesis, titled "The Religious History of Banias and Its Contribution to an Understanding of the Petrine Confession." It's not found on amazon.com either. If you don't know what the Petrine Confession is, then you are unlikely to appreciate Catholicism's teaching on apostolic succession.)

My flirtation with the United Church of Christ did not come out of a vacuous air pocket, however. (I realize a "vacuous air pocket" is physically impossible, so just humor me.) While at Hardin-Simmons, Dr. Auvenshine encouraged several of us to go hear a series of lectures at the neighboring Methodist school, McMurry College, given by the noted Old Testament scholar Walter Brueggemann. After several nights of listening to Dr. Brueggemann, I remember thinking to myself that I didn't understand a word he said, but whatever he was, denominationally speaking, that's what I wanted to be! I discovered he is a United Church of Christ scholar. Along with a research paper on "homosexuality and ordination" that I wrote just before graduation, which featured the theological perspective of several UCC affiliated ethicists, my spiritual identity was coming into sharper focus. (No, I'm not gay. Not that there's anything wrong with that.)

The next leg of my spiritual/educational journey took me to Baylor University in Waco, Texas. Yes, I know, Baylor is also a Southern Baptist institution, but until the week I moved to Waco I had never even *seen* a United Church of Christ building. I was still nominally Baptist, with Pentecostal/charismatic obstinacy and an obviously developing progressive worldview. However, immediately I called a local UCC pastor, set up an appointment to speak with him, learned that he studied under Dr. Brueggemann at Columbia Theological Seminary—an obvious sign that the universe had paused long enough to lead me to the UCC—and agreed to meet with the South Central Conference minister of the UCC. A few months later I was leading two UCC congregations outside of Waco, including a church in West, Texas. While serving there I often had to tell people I lived near West (comma) Texas, but hailed from West (no comma) Texas. Strangely, West, Texas is located in Central Texas. West, of course, is the site of the infamous fertilizer plant explosion of April 2013. I had very little to do with that.

My choice of study at Baylor was Christian ethics, led by Dr. Dan McGee. I often tell people that the reason I chose to study ethics is because people should study what they don't or can't do very well. As was the case at Hardin-Simmons, I cherished my time at Baylor and profess to have learned many valuable things, 80 percent of which I should not (but do) share from the pulpit on Sunday mornings. But if I had to pinpoint a moment in my journey at Baylor that stands out above all others, it would be my introduction to process theology by Dr. Wally Christian. That's right. His name is Dr. *Christian*.

Dr. Christian loved to tell the story of the first time he told his class that he was a Democrat and that any of his offended Republican students (of which there were many) were free to drop his class at that moment. A young coed approached him after class and asked, "Dr. Christian, do you mean to tell me you are a Democrat *and* a Christian?," to which he replied, "Do you mean to tell me you are a *Republican* and a Christian?" None of that had anything to do with the awkward, yet perhaps fortuitous, name he inherited from his father.

The Skeleton Hat Rack

Although my spiritual identity was just beginning to form, the intellectual side of my spiritual journey was about to get stronger legs. Until this point in my life, I had gone from a simple naïve faith to an intentional quest to deconstruct almost everything I could about the Christian faith. At least subconsciously I had discovered agnosticism, which would come to the surface at times . . . even after a Sunday morning worship experience. I remember a young lady who visited First United Church of West one morning telling me she was an agnostic. My hurried response was, "Agnosticism has more intellectual integrity than any other perspective." One of the older members of my congregation heard me say this but fortunately had no idea what I was saying. I have learned over the years that it is fairly easy to say something many people won't understand, which is why Dr. Shield's advice to refrain from sharing 80 percent of what I learned from the university is largely irrelevant.

Even today, I have absolutely no problem with agnosticism and will often call myself a "Christian agnostic" just so I can see the wheels spinning in people's heads. Not to disrespect Leslie Weatherhead, the author of *The Christian Agnostic*, but what I mean when I call myself a Christian agnostic is that I am someone who would like to be identified with Jesus, as difficult as that is at times, and yet I have no idea what God is like or even if there is a God. I'm just being honest. I am reminded of a question posed to Stanley Hauerwas, the great pacifist theologian: "Dr. Hauerwas, are you a Christian?" His witty and profoundly true response was, "No, and I don't know anyone who is." I have no idea where I heard or read this, and would gladly welcome a phone call from Dr. Hauerwas clarifying his remarks.

My point is that God is way beyond our knowing, which is the most obvious point I or anyone else could make. I liken knowledge of God to knowledge of the identity of a CIA agent. If we were ever to learn who God is, God would have to kill us. To me, having "faith" in God, in the culturally misunderstood sense of "believing" in God's existence, is, if one is completely honest with oneself, a shot in the dark, not much different than believing in the existence of the Loch Ness monster or Bigfoot. I suspect that Jesus sought to point people to the "kingdom of God" more so than God perhaps because he already assumed God's existence without question. The compelling theme of the biblical writers is not to believe in God's existence; it is to get with God's program as it is articulated in the most enlightened parts of the Scriptures and through the tradition that has developed in both Western and Eastern religious traditions. There's nothing that says a sincere agnostic can't do that.

Despite my theological skepticism, my introduction to process theology in Dr. Christian's course was enough to stop the bleeding and begin the task of learning to articulate a theological perspective that, if presented in skeletal form, I could hang my spiritual hat on. I'm not an expert on process theology, although I do have a working knowledge of it, suitable for laypersons and country preachers alike. I will now point out some of its more common elements.

Process theology began as a metaphysical philosophy, which simply means it has very little to do with what's on television tonight. Or maybe it does. I have no idea. Alfred North Whitehead (1861–1947) was the philosopher who developed process thought. I suppose a few folks enjoy reading his works. Dr. Christian called Whitehead's book *Process and Reality* the most difficult book to read of all time. That may be hyperbole. Nevertheless, at the risk of exposing my dark side and neglectful parenting techniques, I will acknowledge that when my children used to ask me to read to them a bedtime story I would occasionally pull *Process and Reality* from my shelf, open it to a random page, and begin reading. It sounded something like this: "In the philosophy of organism it is assumed that an actual entity is composite. 'Actuality' is the fundamental exemplification of composition; all other meanings of 'composition' are referent to this root-meaning. But 'actuality' is a general term, which merely indicates this ultimate type of composite unity: there are many composite unities to which this general term applies."[4] Now you know why this has nothing to do with what's on television tonight. Or maybe it does. I have no idea.

A University of Texas theologian, Charles Hartshorne (1897–2000), helped to develop Whitehead's philosophy into a *theology*. (Apparently, reading process theology extends one's life!) Other interesting, if not highly esoteric writers, like Pierre Teilhard de Chardin, thought in process terms, and yet process theology is generally considered to be a Whiteheadian and Hartshornean project. Other important developers of process thought include John B. Cobb Jr. and David Ray Griffin. If you get a chance, read their books. If not, just go *fishing*. You'll see why in a moment.

Fleshing It Out

To help put some skin on process theology I might as well begin with its Wikipedia entry because that's what the curious among you will read first anyway: "For both Whitehead and Hartshorne, it is an essential attribute of God to be fully involved in and affected by temporal processes, an idea that conflicts with traditional forms of theism that hold God to be in all respects non-temporal (eternal), unchanging (immutable), and unaffected by the world (impassible)."[5] This is just a fancy way of saying God and the universe have a very cozy relationship. Process thinkers like to distinguish the "Godhead," which is eternal, immutable, and impassible, from "God," who is in relationship with the universe and is thus affected by what happens. By the way, just so you'll know, "Godhead" doesn't smoke pot. Still, can you imagine how high you and I would get on God's pot? Don't even try.

Traditional (also called "classical" or "orthodox") theists (like the Baptist preacher down your street) like to hang their hats on the "omnis": God's omniscience (all-knowing), omnipotence (all-powerful), omni-benevolence (all-loving), and omni-musicalness (can play every musical instrument in the world at one time). Okay, God hasn't yet revealed an ability to be omni-musical. Or maybe God has. I have no idea. The point is that in traditional theism, *God* is too big. God is too big for God's britches. We'll get to Jesus later.

4. Whitehead, *Process and Reality*, 147.
5. "Process Theology."

In my preaching I often refer to the following notions inspired by process theology. First, much to the chagrin of those who believe human prints have been found imbedded with dinosaur fossil prints, process theology is based on an *evolutionary* model. Just as the universe is expanding, so is God. (No, God isn't fat. Or maybe she is, but I would hesitate to go there.) Just as the universe is in process, so is God. God is part of the evolutionary process. Some thinkers argue that God is "guiding" the evolutionary process, yet I tend to think that God is sort of like a surfer riding the cosmic waves of evolution hoping to ride the pipeline without getting wiped out. (I only know about the pipeline from my wife, a champion surfer in her younger years. As a teenager, she successfully surfed the pipeline in Hawaii, which pretty much trumps everything I have ever done.)

God's role in the evolutionary process is due to God's intense relationship to the universe. From a process perspective, God is not just synonymous with the creation, as pantheism teaches. Pantheism means all *is God.* Humorously, it suggests that God can be in, or is, your couch or dog. (The only thing in my couch is my dog's fleas.) Contrary to pantheism, process theology teaches that the creation or universe is *in God.* Theologians and philosophers refer to this as panentheism. For many monotheists this is far more attractive than traditional theism, which teaches that God is separate from God's creation. Theism is just a hop, skip, and a jump from deism, which teaches that God created the universe and then embarked on an eternal cosmic vacation. "See ya in the afterlife," God said as God set sail for an uninhabitable galaxy. (Keep reading, because later in this book I will tell you when God came back from vacation.)

The practical outcome of this is that *our* experiences are also *God's* experiences. The experiences of the creation are God's experiences, from the macro level to the micro. This is a highly relational theological model, which is generally much more attractive than the God of traditional theism, the God who would rather spit on dirty sinners than hang out with them. What do evangelical Christians like to say? "Sin separates us from God"? Perhaps they should read the Apostle's Paul's process-oriented words in Romans 8: "I'm convinced that *nothing can separate us* from God's love in Christ Jesus our Lord: not death or life, not angels or rulers, not present things or future things, not powers or height or depth, or any other thing that is created."[6]

According to process theology, because God and humanity and all of creation are inseparable from one another, God is very *persuasive.* I don't

---

6. Romans 8:38–39 (CEB). I did not invent italics, yet these are mine.

remember where I read this, but someone has said, "God is not the controlling factor of the universe; God is the persuasive factor." There are many familiar images we can use in order to understand how God's persuasive power might express itself in the God-human-creation relationship. The image I like best is that of *fishing*. Process thinkers often use the word "lure" to describe the way God persuades us. Like my dearly departed great-grandmother who loved to fish, God is constantly luring us to things like goodness and love and justice and compassion, things that characterize Jesus' notion of the kingdom of God. Of course, even the best fisherpersons will *lose* a fish on occasion. At the very least, there is a period of intense struggle as the fish tries desperately to get off the hook. Jesus' time in the wilderness where he was met with very real and human temptations may illustrate Jesus' *squirming* as much as anything else. The aforementioned parable of the prodigal son might also illustrate the intense and sometimes emotional struggle between the One who lures and the ones who are lured. The son spends many years trying to get off the hook, so to speak, but in the end he is lured back to the safety net of his childhood home.

In process theology, God is also like a *music conductor*, directing her orchestra with tempo and emphasis and whatever else conductors do. At first glance, a conductor's job truly seems to be the easiest job in the entire world. Job requirements for a conductor seem to include standing for lengthy periods of time and waving a stick in the air, occasionally pointing and shaking it with an attitude at someone who needs to play their instrument at a higher skill level. Obviously I have no idea what they do and have decided not to even google it. We could also say the process God is like a *lead musician* in a jazz combo. Is there a lead musician in a jazz combo? I'm just asking. Or, to use a better image from the world of music, God is like a *disc jockey*, playing the songs he likes, influencing record sales, bringing smiles to listeners' faces, and yet ultimately is at the mercy of the fickle listener, who may turn off the radio or find another station.

There are myriad images we could use to illustrate God's persuasive influence on us. The obvious point is that persuasion and control are two very different things. In my opinion, the difference here is the theological crux of the matter. People of faith can be divided between those who believe God and God's creation enjoy a disc jockey–listener relationship and those who believe this relationship is more akin to a puppet master–puppet relationship. The difference is crucial. Not that there's anything wrong with puppet masters. Some of my best friends are puppet masters. According to process thinking, God is not the giant puppet master in the sky making us conform to God's "will" or "plan." When God says "Jump," God's creation doesn't necessary jump (although perhaps we should). This is no empty or irrelevant assertion. To suggest that God is in control of the universe, including you and me and all of creation, is to suggest that God is responsible for everything that occurs, from joyful childbirths to the untimely deaths of children. If God is the giant puppet master in the sky, tugging our strings and forcing events to occur, God is responsible for good *and* evil, pleasure *and* pain, order *and* chaos, beautiful rainbows *and* tsunamis. I know no one wants to think about this, but if God is in control of the universe then God is responsible for country music and grass burrs. I shudder as I type these words.

Traditional theism falls into this trap with its emphasis on the omni-God. If God is all-powerful, all-knowing, and all-loving, then why does God cause or allow evil and suffering to occur? This is called the *theodicy* problem. "Theodicy" literally means "the justification of God." In other words, how can we justify God's seemingly uncaring behavior if God can pretty much do anything God damn well pleases? Process theology doesn't fall into this trap because a process God is not an omni-God.

A similar implication in process theology is that God doesn't know *exactly* what will happen in the future, both in the immediate and in the far distant future. If God knows the future, then God is in control of the future, which again poses a problem in terms of evil and suffering. Furthermore, if God is in control of events in history, present and future, then we and the rest of our creaturely brothers and sisters have no *free will*, which is something most of us would like to have, even with the knowledge that nature and nurture both have their deterministic claws in us. Process theology allows room for free will in that it *frees God* from the burdens of dictating events. And yet while God may not know and determine everything that is going to happen, according to process thought God knows all the *potentialities.* That is, God knows everything that could potentially occur in the near and distant future, although God is luring us toward the potentialities that are in line with God's program. I noted earlier that traditional theism's picture of an omni-God presents a God that is *too big.* If God is so all-knowing that God knows everything that is happening and will happen, and if God is so powerful that God can control everything that occurs in history and nature, then by golly, God is one big dude. In process theology, however, God is *even bigger* because, while God doesn't determine everything that happens, God knows everything that could *potentially* happen.

That's a lot more information stored in the divine brain. It seems to me this puts God on a much higher pay scale than traditional theism. (This begs the question: How much *would* we pay God for being God if we were required to do so? An employed God would no doubt be a budget-buster.)

That's Kinda Sexy

While attending Hardin Simmons University I met a middle-aged woman who had gone back to school for a career change. She had been a successful author of romance novels and now she was enrolled in a master's program in religion. She was considering a career change because she could no longer go along with the demands of her publishers. They required a *sex scene* every so many pages in her admittedly formulaic romance stories. She had grown increasingly uncomfortable doing this so she decided to become a Baptist preacher instead. Of course, girls have cooties in Baptist circles, therefore the congregation that called her to their pulpit ended up losing their status as a Southern Baptist church. Kudos to them. Not that there's anything wrong with Southern Baptists. Some of my best friends are Southern Baptists.

In honor of my old friend and because you, the reader, are likely bored out of your ever-loving mind reading about process theology, I would like to insert a mandatory sex scene:

If the space above remains blank that means my publisher is not all that interested in a mandatory sex scene in a work of such high class and distinction. In that case use the space above to jot down questions or comments related to the content of this book so far. By the way, if you bought this book for its high class and distinction, get a refund.

Speaking of sexy, I think the Jesus presented to us through the writings of process thinkers *is* kind of sexy—sexy in the sense that he is highly appealing and attractive. The process Jesus is a Jesus I can relate to, one whose "divinity" is accessible because his humanity is so very much like my own. (Note: I'm still waiting for someone to explain what divinity *is*. I'll pay a hundred bucks for such information.) Until I became fairly versed in process thought, I had been fading from Jesus' fan club. Jesus had been too esoteric. I felt like I was not among the elite few who truly understood the proper Christology. From the very beginning of my academic journey and preaching career, I had wondered why someone so *big* was necessary to intervene in history and put a God-spell on folks when it was clear from my Old Testament studies that God and humanity already had a special bond, as illustrated in the stories of people like Moses, Abraham, Sarah, David, and the prophets. Weren't "God's people" already in the business of revealing God to the world?

Of course, everyone else in the ancient world had their own gods, and they no doubt had their own avatars and gurus and spirit-drenched people creating mythologies and sharing wisdom. However, the God of Israel eventually won the day in the West, leading to the development of the three major monotheistic religions: Judaism, Christianity, and Islam. This didn't happen overnight. My theory is that Yahweh was a god of lesser rank who fought his way up the ladder to become the supreme God, and then, finally, the *only* God. I'm speaking mythologically, of course. In reality, after God created this world she went on a cosmic vacation. Remember deism? Anyway, God's vacation home planet ran out of water. So God decided to come back here to planet Earth, a planet of abundant water, and plant a garden called Eden. According to the Wikipedia entry on "Garden of Eden," *Eden* is believed to be closely related to an Aramaic root word meaning "fruitful, well-watered." Now we know why God went there. Eventually, however, the Garden of Eden was overrun with large, intelligent rat-like creatures that ate the fruit from God's favorite tree. God tried to exterminate them, but without the aid of a solid local Orkin franchise they scurried away. Years later, when the whole region was overrun with these rats, God tried to drown them, but some of them got away by drifting to dry land with other creatures. God finally gave up and decided to just live with the rats as best she could. Eventually, as fate would have it, the rat-like creatures evolved to become human beings.

Okay, enough of the fancy theorizing, so let's get back to Jesus. Perhaps my biggest problem with Big Jesus is that, despite his good intentions, he became (and remains today) an *exclusionary* chap. In orthodox Christianity we have access to God and God's salvation or realm *only* if we believe in a divine Jesus, a Jesus that is set apart from other human beings on this God-damned planet. We are also told we have to believe that Jesus did something—specifically, die on a cross as a blood sacrifice for our sins, or else our sins will remain an albatross around our necks that will accompany us to the depths of hell. (I haven't yet decided if hell is a place of darkness or eternal fire. It can't be both, of course, because the light that emanates from fire gives darkness all kinds of fits. Oh well. No one ever said our theology had to be consistent!)

Process theology explains in rather complex terms that we don't have to think of Jesus in such an exclusionary way. To be extremely simplistic, according to process thinking Jesus just happened to be the right person in the right place at the right time. In other words, I don't think I would have become the savior of the world if I had been born to a teenage virgin in circa 4 B.C.E., but like Jesus I may have died trying. I just don't think I would have been the right person for the job, but Jesus may have been. By the way, my standard response to people who say they believe in a literal virgin birth is "You're shittin' me!" And then I just walk away . . .

People tend to get hung up on the incarnation thing. "Incarnation" means "to give bodily form to." The orthodox position is that Jesus gave bodily form to God, which would make Jesus in essence, well, God. Many Christians understand divinity and humanity to be mutually exclusive substances, which is why the Council of Chalcedon's pronouncement that Jesus is "fully God and fully man" was about as brave as a bull rider with a broken neck. The temptation is to see one substance pushing out another substance from the same limited space. Think *enema*. If Jesus' divinity (whatever that means) pushes out his humanity, we are left with just another funky addition to the mythology of the ancient world: a demigod with an attitude and an agenda. On the other hand, if his humanity pushes out his divinity (whatever that means), we are left with the Dude from *The Big Lebowsky*. (Proof of the connection between Jesus Christ and the Dude is in their use of the word "abides." "The Dude abides," said the Dude. Jesus said, "Abide in me as I abide in you."[7] It's like they're the same dude.) So Christianity managed to both humanize and divinize Jesus at the same time, making him one of the most compelling personalities in human history, which is a gross *misunderestimation*.

Process theology helps us retain both substances—humanity and divinity—because it teaches that humanity is not a closed category.[8] All of us are always open to new transformational experiences, which is a cumulative process. The divinity that we may be in the process of incorporating into our lives doesn't push out our humanity; it enhances it. As C. Robert Mesle suggests, "So when we say we are experiencing God's call and responding to it, we are actually, in the process-relational vision, taking God into ourselves and creating ourselves out of God. God becomes incarnate in our lives. So the ethical affirmation that Jesus responded fully to God's call is transformed into a theological affirmation that Jesus incarnated the divine Word in human form."[9] This "taking God into ourselves and creating ourselves out of God" is something Jesus continued to do throughout his life. Or at least that's what Christians maintain, and you and I have the same option. We can choose to live lives that are open to God's calling and experience transformation to the point that the word "incarnation" applies to many or all of us to one degree or another. The only requirement is to sing "Kumbaya" in beautiful harmony. I'm kidding. No one should have to do that.

However, while this transformational experience in God is open to us all, process theologians make the case that the incarnation of God in humanity took on a unique and special role in Jesus of Nazareth. As the creed says, Jesus was "fully divine and fully human." This is why even today we build churches in his honor and memory and for the sake of forming a community of folks who want to identify with him. We want to be lured in the same direction—without getting crucified of course!

This approach to Jesus' Christology helps us to appreciate and participate in religious pluralism. If all of us can be open to God's lure toward God's realm then we do not have to preclude others from the process of transformation that occurs when people follow, consciously or not, God's

7. John 15:4a (NRSV).

8. Mesle, *Process Theology*, 106.

9. Ibid. Process thinkers argue that our lives are "co-constituted" by our response to God's call or luring. Again, think *fishing*.

persuasive influence in humanity. There have been, and are, many people who ostensibly follow God's lure in their own cultural framework. This gives credibility and validity not only to the followers of the world's major religions, but also to the spiritual seeking that occurs in small and distinct ways in individual lives around the globe. The world is God's pond. We are all being lured into God's realm—a realm that is characterized by justice, peace, love, goodness, compassion, beauty, etc. I know that sounds like a "liberal" realm of God, but I don't think Jesus ever watched Fox News anyway.

So the first way process theology "cuts Jesus down to size" is by proffering the notion that Jesus is not different from you and me in *kind*, but only in *degree*. If someone wants to make the case that Jesus is *more* divine than the rest of humanity, I won't argue with him until I'm blue in the face. I might even nod in agreement. One of my favorite things to do is nod in agreement while listening to people I consider to be dumbasses. It makes me feel all warm and fuzzy inside. However, I might stir the pot by asking him to define "divinity." As far as I know, divinity is not anything that can be proven or experienced with the five senses. To say that something or someone is "divine," other than a general observation that a piece of furniture is "simply divine," is nothing more than a value judgment. It feels like a vacuous statement. Seriously, was Jesus more divine than the Buddha or Gandhi or Maimonides or Susan Sarandon? I don't know how anyone can make a definitive case about such things. (There's just something about Susan . . .)

The second way process theology cuts Jesus down to size is by going in the other theological direction to make the case that "Christ," a translation of the Hebrew word *messiah*, is not so much about a particular individual, namely, Jesus of Nazareth; instead, it is about a larger entity or principle: the "Cosmic Christ." John B. Cobb Jr. suggests the following: "The universal principle of life and light, creation and redemption, which is the presence of God in all things, is what we call Christ. The redemptive, creative activity of God everywhere is what the Christian discerns as Christ."[10] Cobb claims that "it is in Jesus that Christ is made known, is present, and is real."[11] When we look at Jesus through the Gospels we are seeing the Christ principle, the presence of God, as profoundly as we possibly can through the writings of our ancient forbears. This begs the question, however, about whether or

10. Cobb, *Process Perspective*, 37.
11. Ibid.

not and *how* we can see, experience, or sense the Christ principle in and through and around us now. That sounds hard to me.

Incarnation, therefore, occurs in Jesus, in you and me, and throughout "life and light, creation and redemption." This cuts the historical Jesus down to size, no doubt, and yet it also puts him *and us* on a pedestal of value and meaning beyond the scope of rationality, reason, and science. The following quote from Cobb makes me want to join others in a circle and sing that "Kumbaya" song: "God is present in the most literal sense in every creaturely occasion. In human beings, God is the source of novelty, of purpose, of meaning, of openness to others, of freedom, of responsibility, and of much else besides. Far from diminishing our humanity, God is the giver of that humanity. *The more fully God is present, the more fully we are human.*"[12]

That's kind of sexy.

Oh Crap. What Have I Got Myself into Now?

As I stated earlier, my PhD studies focused on the field of Christian ethics, and I would not choose another discipline to study in such a concentrated level even if my life depended on it. Well, that's an overstatement. However, the field of ethics has helped me in this weird journey we call life in ways I can't describe. Well, that's an overstatement too. Most notably, the study of ethics allows me to watch Fox News or listen to Rush Limbaugh and feel smug and superior. I really dig that. Ethics helps me find a way to *be* Christian in a practical sense. I have a measure of confidence that I could answer the question, "What would Jesus do?" in a lot of situations, especially when it comes to war and peace and a rejection of "the myth of redemptive violence." I will define this phrase later when I explore the works of Walter Wink. Stay tuned. In the meantime, put a moratorium on the notion that you can kick your neighbor's ass and call it "Christian."

Still, it was my study of process theology that helped me find a way to be Christian in the classic understanding of faith. I'm not a big faith guy in the sense that I think we can just snap our fingers and have more of it. To me, faith is sort of a natural response to life—a posture of trust—in the face of all the curve balls life can throw our way. Process theology helped to substantiate my faith, to not turn my head in embarrassment when I have a "faith moment," one of those moments when you feel like you are not

12. Ibid, 39. Italics are mine, or, well, I borrowed them.

alone, when something bigger than you and me seems to be loitering in our hearts. (My face just turned red. Damn it.)

I perceive my university studies of the Old Testament, ethics, and process theology as the first three of the five major legs in the academic side of my spiritual journey. (The other two legs, which I will discuss in subsequent chapters, include my study and ever so slight involvement in the search for the historical Jesus and my current flirtation with emergence Christianity.) That is where I stood in the mid-1990s. It took a while to get there, including three college degrees at two different schools over a period of eleven years, all while raising three children. It wasn't easy. While attending Baylor I was called to serve two United Church of Christ congregations. I often needed to supplement my income, so one year I worked as a graduate assistant, drove a school bus morning and evening, and substitute taught in the local school district. Nothing is more humbling for a PhD candidate than driving a school bus in rural Texas on dirt roads.

Graduating from Baylor felt like the end of a long marathon, and yet I knew instinctively that I was just getting started. Certainly in terms of my understanding of Jesus, I was just scratching the surface. My Christology had already run the gamut from the "died for my sins" Baptist Jesus, to the "move out of the way and make room for the Holy Spirit" charismatic and Pentecostal Jesus, back to a more moderate Baptist Jesus who had a thing or two to say about how we should live on this side of eternity, to the "just like me only to a greater degree" Jesus of process theology, to the socially progressive Jesus of mainline Protestantism. So here I was, Sunday after Sunday, preaching from a United Church of Christ pulpit, trying to understand why Jesus seems to appeal to different folks in so many different ways. And truly, all I ever wanted to be was a glorified Sunday school teacher in my one-horse West Texas town while cutting meat in my parents' butcher shop and repeating to myself, "The customer is always right." Now, all I could say to myself after all these years was, "Oh crap. What have I got myself into now?" A person who is knowledgeable about human psychology once told me that I "allow things to happen to me," as if I exercise no choice in important matters pertaining to my life's trajectory. If that's true, then rather than see that as a negative thing I choose to see myself as a very spiritual human being open to the leading—I mean, the *luring*—of the Holy Spirit . . . or something like that.

3

Big Jesus

The God of the Bible is seen in Scripture as Creator, Ruler, Judge, and Savior. His name is Jesus. He is the Creator of the entire world; He Rules over all of creation, all peoples, all cultures, and all religions; he will one day Judge everybody who has ever lived, NOT on if they have been good or bad (he is not Santa Clause) but whether they have repented of sin and have believed in him as Savior and King; and he is the Savior of the world—he is a God who saves.

Jesus is a big God. He is not a little God that lives on a bumper sticker or a little God that is created in our image to justify our actions and the way we want to live. He is a God that demands obedience from his people—his church. He is God of gods and Lord of lords. He is not small. Only small gods live on bumper stickers.[1]

Question: What do Michael Jordan and Jesus Christ have in common?

Answer: Good hang time.[2]

---

1. Gibson, "God Is Too Big." This entire quote was found on the bumper of a Hummer.

2. This joke is actually a product of my sick sense of humor. I expect to receive royalty checks for it someday.

The Napoleon Complex

For most of my childhood and adolescence I was not only slightly built; I was short in stature. It wasn't until my junior year in high school that I grew a few inches. By my senior year I had hit six feet, tall enough to jump center at tip-off a couple of games for my high school basketball team. Our tall guys were hurt or, in the case of one of them, just had no ability to jump. Let the record show, however, that I lost all tip-off attempts. I was no Michael Jordan . . . or Jesus Christ. As I alluded to previously, I was not the most popular guy in town either. I never quite drank enough of the redneck Kool-Aid. When you add all of this together you get a young man who freaking needs *protection*. And I have to say that I was remarkably lucky in that category. Perhaps the only reason I don't have brain trauma today is because I befriended the two biggest dudes in my school. Both were about as unpopular as I was, but nobody messed with them. I mean *nobody*. In track and field, one of them threw the shot put and the other threw the discus. They were both tall and lean and muscular and mean. I don't mean they were mean in the sense of not being nice guys. I just mean they were mean in the sense they were not likely to take any crap from anyone. They were good friends to have. I could tell many stories about these two guys, but I don't want my ass kicked.

Add to my slight build a smart-ass personality and, presto, out pops a French king! Looking back, I don't think there is any doubt that I had a bit of a "Napoleon complex," otherwise known as the "Napoleon syndrome" or "short man syndrome." The Napoleon complex is fairly self-explanatory. It refers to a psychological problem often found in men who are short of stature. In order to compensate for a lack of height, short men will sometimes become overly aggressive. Lack of stature is not the only trigger for a Napoleon complex, however. It is also found in people who feel handicapped or inadequate in particular ways and so will overcompensate in other areas of their lives. For example, while I am no longer short in stature, I am a horrible singer, so I try to overcompensate with superior lip-synching.[3]

---

3 The Napoleon complex is named after Emperor Napoleon I of France. The conventional wisdom is that Napoleon compensated for his lack of height by seeking power, war, and conquest. However, Napoleon was actually above average height for his time period; the average eighteenth-century Frenchman stood at 5'3" and historians have now suggested Napoleon was 5'6". Napoleon was often seen with his Imperial Guard, which contributed to the perception of his being short because the Imperial Guards were above average height. "Napoleon Complex."

I have a theory. Feel free to reject it if you feel your pastor or priest will go into cardiac arrest if you share it with him or her. Here goes: Jesus died an untimely death, thus handicapping the movement he ostensibly began. His early followers, therefore, developed a psychological problem very much akin to the Napoleon complex. Simply put, the messiah was not supposed to die, especially a death that did not occur in the pursuit of political and military liberation of the Jews from Roman occupation. Jesus the messiah was supposed to be Napoleonic in ways other than stature. The people were looking for freedom if not outright conquest. Add to the mix that Jesus died the death of a common criminal and you have the recipe for a major reformulation and reinterpretation of who Jesus was, what he was supposed to do, and what he would become. Jesus himself did not have a first-century version of the Napoleon complex; his followers did. And boy, did they ever overcompensate!

Of course, if the Jesus of first-century Palestine suddenly popped up in our time, he might actually develop a rather severe case of the short man syndrome. Historians tell us that the average height for a Palestinian male of that era was about 5'1". A twenty-first-century Jesus in his original form might shed his "turn the other cheek" philosophy in favor of a "kick ass and ask questions later" approach to conflict resolution. If he is anything like the Gospels describe him, he certainly has the moxie and power to do a lot of irreparable damage to the human race. I'm praying, therefore, that the second coming is just a bunch of hogwash because I would hate to see what an overcompensating Jesus might do. If Jesus does show up in this manner, I suggest that everyone get down on their knees—to pray *and* to look short.[4]

This chapter will summarize the many ways Jesus' followers (ancient and contemporary) have overcompensated for his untimely and unfortunate demise by promoting him to what I'm calling "Big Jesus." Like most of you, I am very familiar with this Jesus. My experience as a minister for twenty-five years has informed me that most people have inherited from their faith tradition a gigantic Jesus of epic proportions. I am almost hesitant to knock him down to size, and if I thought he truly was coming back as a 5'1" man with unlimited powers, I would probably keep my mouth shut. However, regardless of his original stature, Jesus doesn't strike me as the vindictive type. If I pick and choose the stories and parables and short sayings in the Gospels carefully, I discover a gracious man of unlimited

4. See Carr, "How Tall Was Jesus?"

love. I'm not worried one bit. I don't even need my high school chums to protect me.

In the fall of 2012, the popularity of the larger-than-necessary Jesus in American culture became even more evident to me and my wife. For our honeymoon we visited Eureka Springs, Arkansas, home of *The Great Passion Play* and *Christ of the Ozarks*. The latter is a twenty-meter-tall sculpture of Jesus. Other than the fact that his arms are outstretched sans cross, which says to me that the good folks from Arkansas didn't want a Catholic Jesus, theologically speaking, the visual message of this statue is that Jesus is *huge.* By that they mean Jesus is larger than life itself. He cannot be portrayed in human terms. He is even bigger than a Texas-sized Jesus. As a native Texan, I have often wondered if its neighboring states suffer from the short man syndrome as well. Is it possible that Arkansas wanted to make Jesus as big as possible to rival anything Texas might produce? Jesus may have been a small man, relative to our time and place, but the church needed and still needs Big Jesus. Even as the church grew in size and power, Jesus grew right along with it.

Grief Therapy

I have probably officiated at well over one hundred funerals in my career as a parish minister. I have said prayers at the gravesides of some of the most wonderful people I have ever met, and I have done the same for people I would have preferred not marry my daughters. I have spoken words of comfort beside the caskets of corporate executives and a mafia hit man. (I can't tell you the identity of the hit man because then someone would have to kill me and everyone who reads this book.) I have eulogized for future saints and former sinners. The variety of folks for whom I have officiated at their funeral is rainbow-like in its scope. However, the one thing almost all of my funerals have had in common is that the dearly departed is remembered more fondly in death than they were experienced in life. A general principle of a funeral or memorial service is that the survivors remember all the good stuff—even with exaggeration at times—and lay aside all the negative memories at least for the time being. It's called "paying respect." If anything negative is said about the deceased loved one, it is usually said in jest. Rarely do ministers or family members speak with pure honesty about the deceased.

Years ago, Elizabeth Kubler-Ross taught us that people generally go through a five-stage process in the face of their own impending death or the death of a loved one.[5] The five stages in order are denial, anger, bargaining, depression, and acceptance. My educated guess is that the more time survivors have in preparation for the death of their loved one, the more accurate the eulogies will be at the funeral or memorial service. This is because the survivors have more time to travel through these five stages and get to the desired destination of acceptance. Acceptance equates to more accuracy and truthfulness. There is less outwardly expressed grief at a service for someone who has gone through a relatively lengthy dying process, therefore "cooler heads will prevail." A more accurate assessment of the merits of the loved one will be reflected in the words of the participants. On the other hand, if someone dies quickly and suddenly, especially as a relatively young person, the funeral service will be marked by intense emotionality and elevated words of remembrance. No expense will be spared at these funerals, largely because the survivors are reeling from the loss of a loved one and cooler heads are not to be found. I would hate to think that funeral home directors take advantage of people in such an emotional state because I know the funeral home business is not about making money; it's about . . . okay, well, never mind.

This leads to my second theoretical explanation for the elevated words used to describe Jesus soon after his death and up to the present age. I should inform the reader that I am not a trained therapist, but it's a lot of fun to throw crap on the wall to see what sticks. My second theory is that the New Testament was written largely as an exercise in *grief therapy*. Think about it. Their beloved Jesus had died. It was an untimely, nonsensical, and sudden death. I know he lingered a little while on the cross before he expired, and yet in relative terms his followers and family didn't even have time to get past the first stage of denial in Kubler-Ross's scheme. Jesus never even got to have a funeral, for God's sake! Even if his body was privileged to enter a burial place, his followers soon discovered an empty tomb, which, before the mythology of a resurrection takes over, denotes a stolen body. John Dominic Crossan, however, suggests the body of Jesus wasn't physically raised on Easter morning, because he was probably taken down from the cross and eaten by stray dogs. Not to sound gross or irreverent, but this would mean the dogs were the first recipients of Holy Communion. Just saying.[6]

5. See Kübler-Ross, *On Death and Dying*.
6. Crossan, *Jesus*, 158.

Of course, these days when someone dies—even an untimely, nonsensical, or sudden death—we don't usually assume their body will come back to life and save the world. We may struggle with denial and anger for a few days or weeks, yet few of us believe our loved ones were on the fast track to Messiah-hood. Therefore, even if our eulogies reflect only the more positive aspects of their lives, we are unlikely to elevate them to a status that exceeds humanity.

Jesus, however, was and is a different story. Even before he died there seems to have been elevated expectations about him, particularly in terms of the long-awaited Jewish messiah. Add to that the fact that Jesus lived and died in a pre-scientific era. What these people lacked in rational skepticism they made up for with a surplus of naivety. The myth of dying-and-rising gods was as believable to adults then as the myth of Santa Claus is to children today. An emotional reaction to Jesus' death was almost guaranteed to elevate him to mythological, even god-like status. The question for us in the twenty-first century is whether or not we can finally make our way through the five stages of grief and learn to accept Jesus for who he truly was: a prodigal son who found God.

Near Death Experience

So the question is not so much who Jesus thought he was, although that is a relevant question. The question that is more relevant for us is who the early Christians thought Jesus was. And while we are at it we might as well ask ourselves the same question. Ever since I participated in an archaeological excavation at biblical Caesarea Philippi in 1988 (modern-day Banias) I have been fascinated with the question Jesus asked his followers: "Who do people say that the Son of Man is?"[7] In my master's thesis I made the argument that many of the locals in the area would have connected Jesus with the Greek god Apollo. (As one bystander said to Jesus, "Sir, I knew Apollo, and you are no Apollo." Jesus won the election anyway.) Perhaps we should be more concerned with what Jesus said and did than with questions about his identity—and go and do likewise. Maybe that will be my next book, because God's knows no one else has ever written a book about what Jesus said and did . . .

As you can probably guess, I have a problem with the traditional ways Christians have understood who Jesus was (and *is*, because, you know, he

7. Matthew 16:13 (NRSV).

52

allegedly came back from the dead!). Our view of Jesus has changed and evolved over the last two thousand-plus years. There is much variety in our understanding of him. The development of Christology through the ages is a rich and fascinating phenomenon. If you want to blow your mind, for example, read Jaroslav Pelikan's 1985 book, *Jesus Through the Centuries: His Place in the History of Culture*. According to this wonderful book, Jesus has filled a lot of "roles" in various human cultures. In my native West Texas, for instance, Jesus is best imagined as a rodeo clown—the one who saves fools from bullhorns up the ass. The fact that Satan has horns is a totally unrelated subject. And no, Pelikan never mentions the rodeo clown Jesus.

For the sake of simplicity, most Christians believe Jesus' "essence" falls somewhere along the divine-human continuum. As the Council of Chalcedon declared in 451 CE, "Jesus was truly God and truly human." This council occurred before Wal-Mart was available in every city and village, so folks had plenty of time to speculate about such esoteric matters. Even today, however, Christians differ on which side of the divine-human continuum they prefer. Traditional or "orthodox" (i.e., "right belief") Christians prefer to emphasize Jesus' divinity, whereas others (unorthodox?) emphasize Jesus' humanity. And of course there are those who grasp for the middle of the continuum. (We call these folks "moderate fence-riding tip-toeing wishy-washy flip-floppers.")

"High Christology" is the term we use for an emphasis on Christ's divinity, usually at the expense of his humanity. When I am discussing high Christology, I usually prefer to call Jesus "Christ," a title that effectively moves Jesus away from his historical reality. I will distinguish between the "Christ of faith" and the "Jesus of history" with more detail below. People who stress the divinity of Christ over his humanity will put a lot of stock in claims about his union with God and his miracles. And if you ask those who prefer a high Christology which is the best of the four Gospels to read, they will tell you without blinking an eye: the Gospel of John. John's Gospel, written much later than the Synoptic (i.e., "seeing together") Gospels (Matthew, Mark, and Luke), reminds me of a contemporary Near Death Experience (NDE). John had a heart attack, lost blood flow to the brain for a few minutes, and came back from his NDE to tell us that "in my Father's house are many dwelling places."[8] That's a big house. On the other hand, those Christians (and yes, they are Christians) who emphasize Jesus' humanity, known as "low Christology," will stress Jesus' suffering and his personal

8. John 14:2 (NRSV).

struggles. These folks prefer to read Mark and Luke. Moderates, I suppose, spend all day reading Matthew's Gospel arguing about whether or not a virgin can get pregnant. (They can, but only if the bathwater is completely full of semen.)

My view is that there is more integrity in a Christology that points to the low side of the continuum. For a variety of reasons, the orthodox position, while giving lip service to both Jesus' divinity *and* humanity, seems much more passionate about the high side of the continuum. (Studies also show that high Christology folks are much more likely to own guns, so those of us on the low side of the christological spectrum are less passionate about our views *for a very good reason.*) Other than my two previous theories—explaining the need to postulate a "Big Jesus" because of Christianity's Napoleon complex, and because it hasn't quite navigated the grief process—a third theory can be summed up in one word: *fear.* Specifically, the church fears that if Jesus is lessened or diminished in theological stature then we might as well kiss the church goodbye. After over two thousand years of presenting a messianic superman to the world, the thought of swallowing ecclesiastical pride and allowing the integrity of a lower Christology to win the day is too much to bear.[9]

With a little paraphrasing, Iris Dement's song "Our Town" could be the church's anthem if the church decides to take a different course of action: "Go on now and kiss it [our town] goodbye, but hold on to your lover because your heart's bound to die." Yes, we might have to kiss the church goodbye if we decide to bring Jesus back down to earth as the prodigal son par excellence. Many hearts would surely die even as we held on to Jesus our lover with more integrity and realism. I suspect, however, that the church would actually bounce back from its christological NDE with renewed vigor. The sky would be the limit, as they say in my native West Texas. So I sing along with Iris, "Go on now and say goodbye to our town, to our town. Can't you see the sun's settin' down on our town, on our town, good night." And good riddance.

Jesus vs. Jesus

My favorite thing about my parents' grocery store was the magazine rack. The rack stayed up until the local Baptist mothers realized the bare-breasted

9. For comparisons between Jesus and Superman, see Sandlin, "Superman vs. Jesus." Question: If Lois Lane is Mary Magdalene, who the heck is Lana Lang?

magazines on the top shelf were not *National Geographic* issues. Comic books graced the bottom shelf, easily accessible for small children. In my youth I read a lot of comic books because at the end of the month I was allowed to take home the unsold comics, including some of my favorites: *Superman, Batman and Robin*, and *The Archies*. (To this day I wonder whether Archie picked Betty or Veronica. He was obviously a sex addict.) I spent hours sitting next to my German shepherd dog, Judy, reading comic books and drinking bottled Coke. Because I was a very sophisticated comic book reader, however, my absolute favorite was *Mad* magazine. Every month I would hope there would be at least one issue of *Mad* still sitting on the rack when the new editions arrived.

My favorite part of *Mad* was the infamous *Spy vs. Spy* comic strip written by Cuban exile Antonio Prohias. The comic strip features two spies who look like identical twins with unflattering noses, except for the fact that one is dressed in white and the other in black. Oddly enough, I don't recall that the white spy was portrayed as the good guy or the black spy as bad. I hate it when Cuban expatriates defy American cultural stereotypes! The genius of *Spy vs. Spy* is that the two spies never speak and yet the "reader" understands what is happening. It's all action and body language. The two spies seem not to care much about gathering information for their respective governments; they just want to do everything they can to get rid of the other one, using a variety of booby traps. Sometime the white spy would win, other times the black spy would come out on top.

In a very similar way, the church has given us "Jesus vs. Jesus," only with a little more color variation. To which should we be loyal? Typically these two oppositional characters are described as the "Jesus of history" and the "Christ of faith," terminology that was coined by Martin Kahler in 1892. Both are found in the New Testament. The Jesus of history is supported primarily through the fields of archeology and history, whereas the Christ of faith is found in the creeds of the early church councils and all throughout the developing Christian tradition. Kahler noted that there are two German words for "history." *Historie* refers to the science of assembling historical facts about Jesus of Nazareth. Kahler believed this was an impossible endeavor. *Geschichte*, on the other hand, looks at the historical impact of Jesus primarily from a *faith* perspective. Hence, the Christ of faith is all we can really talk about.[10]

---

10. Bessler, *Scandalous Jesus*, 1.

Low Christology focuses more on the attributes of the Jesus of history, the flesh-and-blood Galilean Jew who lived in the early part of the first century. Of course, if it weren't for Jesus our "first century" would be very different. For example, I am writing this in the Jewish year 5773. But since I'm Scotch-Irish German English with a healthy dose of Native American blood coursing through my veins, I have no idea what year it is. I suppose it's somewhere around 13,800,000,000 ABB (After the Big Bang).

High Christology, in contrast, relies primarily on the Christ of faith, a character that is the product of an ongoing theological spin. Years ago, one of my congregants referred to the Apostle Paul as a "spin master." This gentleman was unfortunately a rabid hockey fan, which made me question his sanity. But I digress. Christians have "spun" Jesus ever since he (allegedly) rose from the dead. After that, people started writing nice things about him. (Remember, they were grieving his death!) The Christ of faith not only rose from the dead; his death has "salvific efficacy." (So will mine; just you wait and see.) The Christ of faith is a divine incarnation of God, the one who gives new meaning to the "Anointed One" (Christ or Messiah) of the Hebrew tradition. The Christ of faith can do whatever the heck he wants to in terms of nature miracles, healings, and exorcisms. The Christ of faith is the "savior" who will come back to earth, preferably in our lifetime, and bring about a New Age. The Christ of faith requires our "belief" in him, along with our repentance. The Christ of faith is too big, too ubiquitous, too important, and too entrenched in the Christian tradition to fail!

The Jesus of history doesn't have a prayer against this dude. This is where the *Spy vs. Spy* analogy breaks down. In the comic strip, the two characters are equal adversaries. In the history of Christology, however, the Christ of faith is a giant compared to the Jesus of history, who is more like a shepherd boy. (And we all know what happens when a shepherd boy confronts a giant . . . oh wait.) What the average churchgoer doesn't realize is that we are in a historic struggle between the Jesus of history and the Christ of faith. The two characters are squaring off in a heated battle of wits and determination. It may come down to who has the best booby traps!

As a preaching pastor, I have been in the trenches of this historic struggle between the two Jesus' for well over two decades. I have noticed two things about myself and about how this plays out, even in theologically diverse congregations of the United Church of Christ. First of all, the majority of my sermons over the years have stemmed from the narratives of the Gospels, typically from the Synoptics (Matthew, Mark, and Luke), but occasionally from the Gospel of John. I am primarily a "lectionary" preacher. The lectionary is a three-year cycle of readings from Scripture that typically includes selections from the Old Testament, Psalms, the New Testament Epistles, and the Gospels. Alternative selections are frequently included as well. Unlike many lectionary preachers I prefer to focus on just one of the readings per Sunday so that I don't make "forced" connections between two or more readings from different parts of the Bible. The aforementioned Dr. Wally Christian from Baylor University also suggested that the use of the lectionary might keep my colleagues and me from pet-peeve preaching. By following the lectionary I am forced to grapple with Scripture passages that I would prefer to ignore. Of course, the lectionary conveniently and practically ignores much of the available Scriptures, so it is a good idea on occasion to escape from the limitations of the lectionary and practice what I call "Star Trek serminating" . . . boldly going where no one has gone before.

I have developed into a primarily "narrative" or "postliberal" preacher. This is the practice of focusing on narrative presentations of the Christian faith rather than delivering a set of propositions derived in a systematic way from the Scriptures. Furthermore, I could care less if a story in the Bible is historically accurate or not. This is an argument between old-fashioned liberals and conservatives. As a *post*liberal (because, yes, I am informed by liberal theology), I am more interested in the meaning of the story rather than its historicity. In doing so I am fully aware that my social location influences the meaning of the story that I present to my congregation. In other words, when I preach the congregation is hearing "The Gospel According to Jimmy." At least I admit it.

I have noticed, but can't confirm, that mainline Protestant clergy preach primarily from the Gospels and therefore focus, wittingly or not, on the Jesus of history. These sermons tend to focus more on ethics (what to *do*) than theology (what to *believe*). In contrast, evangelical preachers tend to use the New Testament Epistles in order to deliver theological propositions, often about Jesus and his salvific efficacy. For evangelicals it is very important to be orthodox, to have the "right beliefs," because, well, failure to do so could mean that one's life will end up in a roast. My greatest desire is to be "roasted" upon my retirement, yet not in the way my evangelical siblings occasionally wish for me.

Christianity is in a knock-down-drag-out fight between the Jesus of history and the Christ of faith. There is a lot of baggage that accompanies each of these Jesus'. In my opinion, focusing on the Jesus of history (low Christology) leads to the consideration of a lifestyle and social ethic that at least partially subverts the values of humanity in all corners of the globe. The Jesus of history "lures" us toward such values as justice and peace, compassion and mercy. On the other hand, emphasizing the Christ of faith (high Christology) brings the church primarily into the business of beliefs, doctrines, creeds, and rigid personal morality. A lot of people are walking around out there referring to themselves as "Christians," and many of us, including myself, would prefer not to be lumped in with those who use the word for purposes other than what Jesus himself wanted. Or at least that's my opinion, and we all know what people say about opinions. (People say opinions are like belly buttons or the singular bodily orifice on their backsides: everyone has one. By the way, my ears always perk up when I hear someone say, "Everyone is entitled to their own opinions, but not to their own facts," which is usually stated by someone who has very strong opinions. My opinion is that living in a free country entitles all of us to our own facts as well as our own opinions, which is why we have both a belly button and an anal orifice.)

I can see why Anne Rice, the famed vampire book writer who re-turned to Catholicism in her fifties, left the church in 2010 because, as she sees it, the church is largely anti-gay, anti-feminist, anti-artificial birth control, anti-Democrat, anti-secular humanism, anti-science, and anti-life. (Yes, but the church obviously loves a blood thirsty, vampire-like God, so what's her problem?[11]) By the way, Anne still loves Jesus; it's just the church she rejects. For a similar view of the church, note Gandhi's famous quote, "I like your Christ, but I do not like your Christians. Your Christians are so unlike your Christ." Or, more importantly (because Gandhi is dead), listen to another Iris Dement song, "Wasteland of the Free," where she refers to the hypocritical preachers out there: "They say they are Christ's disciples; they don't look like Jesus to me." And they're relatively taller as well.

A Caricature of Himself

One area in which the Jesus of history and the Christ of faith often overlap is the claim in the New Testament that the flesh-and-blood Jesus of Naza-reth was able to perform miracles, including exorcisms and healings. There is little doubt in my mind that Jesus had unique charismatic gifts that he

11. See Rice, "Reasons for Quitting Christianity."

could use to gather and woo a crowd, relate to the common people of his day through parables and aphorisms, and elicit a response of either adoration or condemnation. There was just something about Jesus. We already know there's something about Mary . . . and Susan Sarandon.

The presence of miracles, exorcisms, and healings in the Gospels can be explained by one simple fact: people in the ancient world believed in the existence of these phenomena more readily than people today, mainly *out of necessity.* There are still people who believe in such things today, especially in Third World countries, and even in First World countries such as our own. (I'm constantly encountering people who believe I need an exorcism.) The people in the ancient world needed to believe that there were ways to control nature, and heal the mentally ill (exorcisms) and physically ill. Imagine how terrifying these events were in a day before such "miracles" as Doppler radar, psychiatric medication, and surgery. Since there were other people walking around with reputations that claimed capabilities that exceeded the limitations of reality, there were more than a few followers of Jesus, before and after his death, who testified to his even more pronounced capabilities to do these things.

Personally, I have trouble believing Jesus did anything more than calm down a few mentally unstable people who hung out at cemeteries or provide comfort to a few lepers who constantly felt "picked on" (sorry, I couldn't help that). I can see, however, how his reputation in that time and place could expand. I admit I have been ruined by the likes of David Hume, who said, "no testimony is sufficient to establish a miracle, unless the testimony be of such a kind, that its falsehood would be more miraculous, than the fact, which it endeavors to establish."[12] David had a way with words! In other words, I would almost have to see it to believe it.

In some ways, through the testimony of the church Jesus has become a caricature of himself. A caricature is "a representation, especially pictorial or literary, in which the subject's distinctive features or peculiarities are deliberately exaggerated to produce a comic or grotesque effect."[13] I would stop short of saying the exaggerations about Jesus in terms of his wonder-working power are "comic" or "grotesque," and yet I can say that Jesus, through the testimony of the early church, became a big deal. Of course, to claim that Jesus was an exorcist is to assume that demons actually exist.

12. Hume, *Enquiry,* "Of Miracles," part 1.

13. "Caricature," The Free Dictionary, online: http://www.thefreedictionary.com/caricature.

They do, but they only live among (in) people in warmer climates such as the American Deep South. This has nothing to do with Southerners, per se, but everything to do with the demonic fear of snow . . .

The Sinful Messiah

Another area in which the Jesus of history and the Christ of faith overlap is in Christianity's claim that Jesus was the Jewish Messiah. Obviously, it is the voice of faith that refers to someone as Messiah or Christ, but at least to a certain degree we can inspect his messianic credentials from a historical perspective. Perhaps I am somewhat qualified to do this. After all, while I have never personally met a messiah, I came really close once upon a time. I almost met David Koresh of Waco, Texas. (Well, not really. However, I almost met Jimmy Carter. In 1992, the Clintons and Gores stopped in Waco for a campaign event on the banks of the Brazos River. While standing in the crowd waiting for them to arrive, a man who looked just like Jimmy Carter stood next to me. He was Ed Beheler, the "number one international Jimmy Carter look-alike." Thank goodness he was also a Democrat because that would have confused me.)

The date was February 28, 1993. I was traveling with a few friends from my two Waco-area congregations to a UCC church in Fort Worth for my Ecclesiastical Council (EC). In the United Church of Christ an EC entails standing before a group of folks in one's association—clergy and laity alike—and making a presentation of one's spiritual journey and theological perspective for the purpose of seeking ordination status. I was both excited and nervous because as a former Southern Baptist I knew that my EC would be met with cautious skepticism. There was and is a concern in UCC circles about "steeplejackers," conservative ministers and lay persons who infiltrate the denomination in order to lead an autonomous congregation out of the United Church of Christ. The more technical term for a steeplejacker is "asshole," but once again, I digress. My fear was validated when some of the more liberal ministers in the association began to ask rather difficult questions. They were surely thinking, "This guy was educated by Baptists. There is no way he is theologically sophisticated enough to be a mainline Protestant." On the other hand, the conservatives in the audience were just as critical, thinking, "This guy was educated by the Baptists, but now he wants to be UCC. He must be a flaming liberal." (Funny, both sides were correct in their assessment of me.) I must have appeased both sides with long-winded answers grounded in process theology, however, because I was cleared for ordination, which finally took place on May 1, 1993. But I digress yet again.

The other event of significance on February 28, 1993, was the siege of the Branch Davidian compound near Mt. Carmel, Texas, a few miles northeast of Waco. The Branch Davidians were led by Vernon Howell, alias David Koresh. I just happened to live about five miles as the crow flies from their compound. The Bureau of Alcohol, Tobacco, and Firearms (ATF) had been investigating for several months allegations of child molestation and stockpiling of illegal weapons at the compound. From my understanding of the events, relayed to me by professors who were in communication with the ATF at the time, the latter wanted to pick up Koresh on Monday, March 1, while he was out on his morning jog. On Saturday, however, the local newspaper, the *Waco Tribune-Herald*, ran a front-page headline that read, "The Sinful Messiah," along with a large headshot of Koresh. This must have tipped off Koresh, compelling the ATF to siege the compound on Sunday morning, a day early (or rather, a day late). This was a disastrous move culminating in the deaths of four ATF agents and six Branch Davidians. Eventually, on April 19, all eighty of the inhabitants who remained would die in the flames of the burning compound.

My "claim to fame" is that one day during the siege a gentleman from my congregation drove up to my church in a black Camaro after Sunday morning worship. He owned a local wrecking yard and the ATF were paying him to house the vehicles they were pulling away from the premises of the Branch Davidian compound. He asked me to get in. It was David Koresh's car. No, I never met him, but I rode in his car.

David Koresh had messianic aspirations not unlike many in first-century Palestine—a spiritual warrior-messiah who felt called to lead the Jews to defeat government oppression. Peter Enns refers to this as "plagiarism" on the part of Koresh and the Branch Davidians.[14] I once heard David preach for an hour and a half, his voice recorded on a cassette tape found in his Camaro. He made no sense at all, yet there is no doubt in my mind that he saw himself as the Messiah, the one who would usher in the messianic age. It is not without coincidence that he referred to himself as "Cyrus," the Persian king who helped liberate the Jews from Babylonian Exile in the sixth century BCE. The Jews referred to Cyrus as "the anointed of the Lord,"

14. Enns, "Were David Koresh and the Branch Dividians."

which is another way to refer to the Messiah.[15] The hoped-for Jewish Messiah in ancient Israel was the anointed one of God, a leader descended from the family tree of King David. The Messiah would rule the tribes of Israel and bring in the messianic age. Jesus' inaugural sermon at the synagogue in Nazareth, where he quotes from the book of Isaiah, is generally taken as at least a poetic description of the messianic age: "The Spirit of the Lord is upon me, because the Lord has anointed me. He has sent me to preach good news to the poor, to proclaim release to the prisoners and recovery of sight to the blind, to liberate the oppressed, and to proclaim the year of the Lord's favor."[16]

The reference to the word "anointed," which is closely associated with the Jewish Messiah, would have been a clear signal to his audience of his messianic intentions. There is some debate, of course, whether Jesus was literate or not and therefore whether he read this passage or recited it from memory. (I know, I know. A messiah that can't read? Bite my tongue!) Of course, Jesus died before the world really changed in the direction of messianic expectations. Therefore, his death complicated matters a great deal. The early Christian view that the Messiah would be killed and raised on the third day after death was not a general view at the time, although many Jews believed the messianic age would lead to a "general resurrection of the dead." The fact that only Jesus was raised from the dead did not help to convince all the "Doubting Thomas's" that Jesus was indeed the Messiah. (There was really only one Doubting Thomas in that day, and compared to most us he wasn't much of a doubter. Perhaps his twin was, however.) Whether Jesus understood himself to be the Messiah or not, the early Christians could not help but look back upon Jesus' life and find justification for acknowledging Jesus as the Messiah, the Christ, the anointed one of God. I don't think Jesus ever drank the "messianic Kool-Aid." If he did, he had a radically different view of what it meant to be the Messiah than his contemporaries held. Unlike David Koresh, however, Jesus was not—and couldn't possibly be—a *sinful* messiah. Could he?

Regardless, Jesus' followers were not quite content with the messianic tag. That wasn't quite *big enough*.[17] If the Jesus movement were to continue and prosper, he needed more street cred.

15. "Cyrus the Great."

16. Luke 4:18–19 (CEB).

17. For a good description of the messianic expectations of the first century, see Levine, *Misunderstood Jew*, 56–62.

The Biggie

What was really needed for Jesus' postmortem resume in the early years after his death was something that would perk up the ears of every open-hearted Jew and Gentile alike. If his death was untimely, negating the messianic claim, then his death needed to be negated as well. Enter the doctrine of the *resurrection*. We can call this doctrine "the biggie." There are an enormous number of Christians who populate the world's pews each and every weekend who are convinced that one must believe in the physical, bodily, corporeal resurrection of Jesus Christ . . . or else. Most Christians assume it is *the* central claim of the Christian faith. They also assume that if the resurrection story is removed from the Christian house of cards the whole enterprise comes tumbling down.

The tension between the Jesus of history and the Christ of faith comes into very clear focus here. From a historical perspective there is no way to verify an empty tomb, a physical presence of Jesus after his death, or even placement in a tomb in the first place. We are pretty sure he died—unless he never lived to begin with, in which case I can just stop writing now . . .

Okay, I'm back, but I'm a little fearful that some of my readers might misunderstand me here. I would never unequivocally deny the resurrection of Jesus the Christ because, quite frankly, I wasn't there, and yet neither can I verify it. All I can really say with as much honesty and integrity as I can muster is that, as I implied earlier, Jesus' death really put his followers in a tailspin. Not only did he die before he could fulfill the messianic expectations of his people; he died in a horrible manner. He died the death of a common criminal.

I am not making the argument, however, that this means the followers of Jesus simply decided to add the resurrection to Jesus' biography to somehow bolster his messianic credentials. N. T. Wright has argued, persuasively in my opinion, that "nobody expected the Messiah to be raised from the dead, for the simple reason that nobody in Judaism at the time expected a Messiah who would die, especially one who would die shamefully and violently."[18] There is no way to overemphasize the sheer confusion and panic that must have ensued among Jesus' followers after his death. Was he really the Messiah? If they killed him, will they kill us? With Jesus gone, do we lose our free passes to the Creation Museum in Kentucky?

---

18. Wright, *Resurrection of Jesus*, 17.

After much thought and reflection, and without the aid of halluci-nogens, I have narrowed the question of the historical veracity of the resurrection down to three possibilities. (Obviously there are more than three possible explanations of the resurrection, but I have to go pee. Also, although I am already quite a few pages into this book, I have to add the disclaimer that this is not meant to be a scholarly endeavor. But you already knew that.) The first possibility is that it really happened. And if it did hap-pen then "Katie bar the door" because our understanding of the nature of reality is in trouble! (Katie must have been one tough gal.) Obviously, from a scientific perspective our understanding of reality changes constantly, although rarely as radically as one day thinking dead people do not come back to life after three days to the next day thinking they do.

Second, perhaps Jesus had a Near Death Experience, which was ex-tremely rare in a prescientific age because of the lack of modern medical treatment. We can exclude this because of its extreme unlikelihood. Third, even if Wright is correct in saying that no one was looking for a Messiah who would die and rise from the dead, that doesn't mean there were no theologically inventive and edgy people in that day. They must have had their own version of a Nadia Bolz-Weber, the heavily tattooed founding pastor of The House for All Sinners and Saints Lutheran Church in Denver, Colorado. She didn't just come out of the blue. Or maybe she did. I have no idea. The Apostle Paul also comes to mind. As Thomas Sheehan pointed out in his book *The First Coming*, Paul's view was that Jesus was exalted at his resurrection. Listen to Paul the "spin master": "He [Jesus] was pub-licly identified as God's Son with power *through his resurrection* from the dead, which was based on the Spirit of holiness. This Son is Jesus Christ our Lord."[19]

My point is a simple one. Something needed to jumpstart the messi-anic age. If the designated Messiah had died, leaving most people in serious doubt about his credentials, then, logically speaking, he needed to come back to life. Unless they were willing to let the movement die, this became the best option on the table. So the question for me is not whether he actu-ally rose from the dead or not—that's a liberal/conservative argument. It's not an argument a historian can make unless one resorts to faith. Other than the question of what the resurrection *means*, the most relevant ques-tion we can ask is why and when his followers begin to acknowledge the resurrection as an event. Did they huddle together a few days after Jesus'

19. Romans 1:4 (CEB). Paul didn't write with italics, so I guess these are mine.

death and think up a sinister plot to mess with people's minds? Did the New Testament writers introduce the idea several decades after his death, or did they merely jot down what had been passed down to them through word of mouth?

In summary, Jesus either (a) was resurrected in the literal sense of coming back from the dead, (b) had a Near Death Experience and eventually recovered from his wounds, or (c) the New Testament writers made the whole thing up. Of course, they could have been smarter than us and knew they were writing *metaphorically*. Other options include the resurrection as spiritual but not bodily, the possibility that Jesus' body was stolen, and the possibility that Jesus' body never made it to the tomb in the first place (and was eaten by the wild dogs). In an empirically oriented world such as ours, the notion that the New Testament writers conjured up the resurrection is much easier to digest than the others. John Shelby Spong, one of the most outspoken critics of traditional Christianity, said, "If we insist that Easter's truth must be carried inside . . . a literal framework, we doom Easter's truth to the death of irrelevance."[20]

Relevant or not, Christians will continue to believe that Jesus rose from the dead, either in body or spirit, literally or metaphorically. This sets Jesus apart from most of the other dying-and-rising gods of the ancient world, who not only have faded into oblivion, but whose credentials come nowhere close to the man from Nazareth.[21] In other words, Jesus has proven to be a big deal . . . and yet a resurrected Messiah was still not "biggie" enough. After all, upon further reflection, his *death* had to mean something, right?

Taking One for the Team

I had my one shining moment back in the early 1990s at Baylor University in Dr. Christian's class on historical theology. Allow me to set the scene. We had been discussing the doctrine of "plenary substitutionary atonement," which basically means "Jesus shed blood and died for your sins so you better get with the program and believe it . . . or else." (Have you ever noticed how many "or elses" there are in traditional religion?) There are variations on this theme, however, atonement theory generally asserts that dirty rotten sinners (i.e., bathed and unbathed human beings) can be reconciled to God

20. Spong, *Resurrection*, 291.

21. See Daniel, "Busting the Dying and Rising God Myths."

because Jesus died on the cross. Yep, the world's largest religion teaches that God needed a blood sacrifice so that we can keep saying naughty words and fudging on our taxes. Or, to put it in contemporary parlance, Jesus "took one for the team."

In traditional Christianity reconciliation means that our sins are forgiven. Of course, because I am who I am (no, I'm not "I AM" in the sense of being God) I'm always seeking clarification about which sins are forgiven. All sins? Sins from the past? Future sins? Do I have to ask for forgiveness or does God already know what I'm thinking? Do I have to believe that Jesus died for my sins? What about those who never heard of Jesus? What about those poor bastards who lived before Jesus? What about children who have heathen parents? You get my point. People assume there is a huge chasm between a holy God and sinful humanity and the only way to bridge that chasm is for Jesus to stretch out his bloody arms to reach from one side to the other. I'm speaking metaphorically, of course. Jesus' arms aren't really that long.

It's not just human beings, however, who might have some skin in this game. If Paul is correct in the eighth chapter of his letter to the Romans, then *all of creation* is waiting like a woman in labor for the hope of reconciliation with God. (Now I know what all the birds are chirping.) This echoes the Hebrew Scripture's hope for the "peaceable kingdom," an eschatological hope that all of creation will live in harmony with one another. Yeah right. Don't hold your breath. (Eschatology, by the way, is that branch of theology that is concerned with the "end times." Therefore, eschatology should be most concerned about the sun burning out, wayward meteors, and hostile aliens. Furthermore, I'm waiting for a good theory that will explain how non-human animals can be forgiven for all their raping, killing, and public farting.) Will the crucified and risen Jesus eventually bring to fruition this peaceable kingdom? Because of the blood of Jesus, people believe there will be a day when "The wolf will live with the lamb, and the leopard will lie down with the young goat; the calf and the young lion will feed together, and a little child will lead them. The cow and the bear will graze. Their young will lie down together, and a lion will eat straw like an ox. A nursing child will play over the snake's hole; toddlers will reach right over the serpent's den."[22] This will never happen because Child Protective Services will make damn sure nobody ever lets their child play over snake holes.

22. Isaiah 11:6–8 (CEB).

Getting back to the human need for reconciliation, Christian theologians have come up with several theories to explain the atonement, or as cutesy preachers like to call it, "at-one-ment":

1. Ransom Theory—Because our sinful ways have put us in so much "debt," Satan held humanity ransom until Jesus came along and dropped the bag at the designated drop spot. Now that Satan has been paid off, we are good to go.

2. Christus Victor Theory—Jesus' death was a "victory" over sin and death. This is like saying a sports team won even though they lost. A moral victory?

3. Moral Influence Theory—Jesus taught us how to live and die. His influence on us leads to our redemption. His death just happened to be the last thing he did.

4. Satisfaction Theory—Jesus' death "satisfied" a pissed off God who was completely fed up with sinful humanity. At this point you will hear the Rolling Stone's song "Satisfaction" as an earworm.

5. Penal Substitution Theory—Jesus served as our "substitute." Through his death on the cross he covered for our sins. A very nice gesture indeed!

There are other theories about the atonement but this gives you an idea about how creative Christians have been in response to Jesus' death. His death simply *had to mean something*.

Now let me get back to my one shining moment. Dr. Christian had given us an exam about atonement theories. One question read as follows: "Do you agree with Peter Anselm's view of substitutionary atonement or Peter Abelard's view of the moral influence theory, and why?" (The story of Anselm and Abelard is interesting; especially the part where Peter Abelard has a love affair with Heloise and her uncle castrates him. Good old Peter took one for the team as well. Consider that a double entendre.) The next day in class, Dr. Christian was going over our exams when he stopped and asked, "How many of you chose Anselm's theory?" Every hand in the class went up *except mine*. I must disclose that at that time I was the only United Church of Christ minister in a school dominated by moderate Southern Baptists and a few scattered fundamentalists. Then Dr. Christian asked if anyone chose Abelard's theory. I shyly and slowly raised my hand, absorbing the icy glares of most of my classmates. A moment later a rush of courage came over me and I asked Dr. Christian which one *he* preferred. He looked right at me, grinned, and said Peter Abelard's name. I'm still basking in the glow of my victory! Anselm, by the way, is also known for the ontological argument or proof for the existence of God, which goes like this: God is "that than which nothing greater can be conceived." Yeah, that definitely proves there is a God.

To be honest I don't know which theory of atonement is correct, or even if any of them are necessary. We only need atonement *if* our problem is sin and separation from God. At this point in my life, I feel drawn toward the Eastern perspective that the problem of humanity is a lack of awareness or mindfulness, and the solution is therefore enlightenment. (Practically speaking, the problem of "American" humanity is the manufacture, sale, and usage of too many damn guns, but I digress once again.) It's easier, however, to pound the pulpit when I'm talking about sin. Still, the progression of Jesus' growing status is clearly evident throughout the New Testament. A wonderful teacher with charismatic gifts is tagged as the Messiah, and then he dies an untimely and shameful death. His followers go into spin mode, creating a fantastic story that includes his resurrection from the dead, his atoning death, and even a future scenario when Jesus *returns*. I just hope he waits until I'm finished watching all of the *Mad Men* episodes.

Return of the Jesus

I have never been a fan of the *Star Wars* movie franchise, primarily because I don't like its bland morality tale of good versus evil or, for the visual learners among us, white versus black," unless they are equally good or bad, such as the spies in *Spy vs. Spy*. Nor do I enjoy its bland theology summarized in the unimaginative blessing, "May the force be with you." Excuse me, but I can get more inspiration out of an electrical socket. However, as I revealed in chapter 1 in my discussion about Jesus' autobiographical parable of the prodigal son, I am always inspired by someone's *return*. Therefore, *Return of the Jedi* might warrant a reviewing someday. (Oh wait, it's not on my bucket list. I just checked. Never mind.) Just so you will understand my psychological state at the present time, I will admit that I tear up every time I hear General Douglas MacArthur telling the Philippines "I shall return" or hear Arnold the Terminator delivering a relatively large slice of his limited movie dialogue, saying, "I'll be back." I also bawl like a baby when an aging athlete makes a comeback.

The "second coming" of Christ elicits an emotional response from me as well. It brings back memories (nightmares really) of reading Hal Lindsey's *The Late Great Planet Earth* and tacking "end times" charts on my bedroom wall. My flirtation with the Parousia only lasted a few years, however—just long enough to burn all of my record albums because I was convinced that Jesus would not think too highly of my teenaged fascination with Led Zeppelin's *Houses of the Holy*. Fortunately, I escaped from my prison of superficial piety and borderline insanity long before the *Left Behind* series began to dominate Wal-Mart's bookshelves. Even if the Bible leaves a few eschatological hints about some future "day of the Lord," "judgment day," or "second coming," I just couldn't figure out *why*. If God has allowed this planet and its inhabitants to evolve for so long, and if God went to all the trouble of sending his "Son" to die for our sins, then why upset the applecart? Why not just let the chips fall where they may?

In the end (no pun intended), I have no use for end-of-the-world scenarios. I like to tell people I believe in "pan-millennialism," which means, "Whatever pans out is good enough for me." Nevertheless, I guess looking for Jesus' return beats having to save the environment from unsustainability . . . So, is Jesus coming back for us someday when the head angel blasts God's trumpet and then a bunch of dead people pop up out of their graves?[23] Give me a break.

The Christinator

I hope what I am about to say doesn't upset Robert Culp and Bill Cosby, who entertained the entire galaxy from 1965 to 1968 with their television show *I Spy*. (I say "the galaxy" because my friends on PNYgrio34[24] watched the show fanatically. They even started playing tennis, which is difficult to do when your eyes are in the back of your head and your head is located in the belly button, which is located . . . I better not say it.) After the identical twins in *Spy vs. Spy*, however, my favorite spy has got to be Perry the Platypus on the cartoon series *Phineas and Ferb*. My son got me hooked on the simple elegance of this series, which follows a standard plot system. There are running gags in every episode, such as Phineas answering a question about whether he is too young to be doing the things he is doing: "Yes, yes I am." This has become my standard answer every time someone

23. 1 Thessalonians 4:16.
24. Not an actual planet.

asks me if I am the center of the universe. Cracks me up every time. In every episode, Phineas' sister, Candace, expends all of her energy trying to catch her two brothers doing things that only *gods* can do. (Of course, it's a cartoon, and many of the characters in cartoons seem to have divine qualities to one degree or another. For example, there seems to be no way to kill a bunny rabbit or a roadrunner in cartoon land.) For my money, nothing beats the sheer creative entertainment of watching a pet platypus disappear for the day because he is secretly a spy, "Agent P," working for the OWCA (Organization Without a Cool Acronym), trying his best to stop an evil scientist named Dr. Heinz Doofenshmirtz. The latter is a highly creative if not impractical inventor who always attaches the suffix "-inator" to the name of his newest gadget. As a fan of the show, I have named myself "the Serminator" and the act of producing a sermon "serminating" (which sounds worse than it really is). Dissimilarly, however, my sermons *never* fall flat like Dr. Doof's inventions. ☺

With a little imagination, it is not too difficult to connect the Christ of faith with many of the attributes of modern cartoon characters, especially their resistance to death. Like Phineas and Ferb, many cartoon characters are almost divine-like. They can do things flesh-and-blood creatures on this planet cannot do. In cartoon land and fantasy fiction animals can speak the King's English, coyotes can live after falling off of cliffs (but not before they suspend gravity for a few moments), and little boys can come back to life in one episode after dying in every previous episode. In almost all *South Park* episodes Kenny dies, and yet there he is in the very next episode. (Oh my God, they killed Kenny!" is exactly what Simon Peter said while he was hiding from the Romans after Jesus died. "Kenny" was Peter's nickname for Jesus.)

Jesus is not exactly a cartoon character, and yet as I implied earlier his powers are almost cartoon-like. We are told he walked on water, stilled the storm, healed the blind, the crippled, and the leper, cast out demons, raised the dead, and walked out of his own tomb. The devil told him he could fall from the top of the temple in Jerusalem and would not be hurt, which is where Wylie Coyote got the notion in the first place. Speaking of demon possession, I often think of the Tasmanian devil in Warner Bros. *Looney Toons*. Taz's Wikipedia page describes his personality thusly: "[He] is generally portrayed as a ferocious albeit dim-witted omnivore with a notoriously short temper and little patience. He will eat anything and everything, with an appetite that seems to know no bounds. He is best known for his speech consisting mostly of grunts, growls and rasps, and his ability to spin like a vortex and bite through just about anything." Strangely, that sounds like some of my church members.

The existence of cartoons in the modern world proves one very important fact: our human limitations are ultimately unacceptable to us. We would love to be able to walk on water and rise from the dead, but we can't, so we invent cartoon and other fantasy characters in order to live vicariously through them. I'm not suggesting we created Jesus out of the need to overcome the natural limitations of our humanity, yet I would argue that in the modern world there is much less need to create such mythological deities because we now have other outlets, namely books, television shows, movies, video games, etc. Jesus became a god because he didn't have a show to go into syndication. I salivate, however, when I think of the possibility of a cartoon featuring Jesus and Peter getting into Batman and Robin–like predicaments and then performing a miracle to get out of their predicament. I would watch that.

Regardless of the motivating factors for creating a divine or semi-divine person in Jesus of Nazareth, the fact is that this is exactly what Christianity has done. We have created Big Jesus. To listen to Christian music and hymnody, both old and new, one would think that Jesus is the most powerful person who has ever lived. To feel this remarkable power just sing the following hymn: "The Power of your love, the power of your grace, the power of your nail scarred hands changed eternal fate. The power of your blood, the power of your word, the power of your life in me, makes me free today." Or just say "The power of Christ compels you" and see what happens to the neighborhood bully. The only reason he wasn't faster than a speeding bullet is because the Jews of the first century didn't have any guns. If they had had guns they would have made mincemeat out of the Romans (as long as the Romans didn't have *bigger* guns).

I know from experience that to question the divinity of Jesus is about as dangerous as riding a bull . . . without a rodeo clown's help. Apparently I did this once, inadvertently, from an East Texas pulpit. I questioned Jesus' divinity; I didn't ride a bull. I had previously allowed an African-American minister with impeccable credentials to fill my pulpit while away on vacation. (I felt like I needed to add "impeccable credentials" because, you know, I can't just say "African-American minister.") This pissed off a few folks, especially one gentleman who had been a "peace officer" in Mississippi during the civil rights movement. He was apparently still angry because some of the African-Americans from his hometown had chased him out of his hometown. When I asked him why they did that, he responded, "I was only following orders." Now, years after that incident, he was telling me that allowing a black man in the pulpit was a "desecration." How sad.

Unfortunately, he wasn't alone in his negativity. Like a festering sore, many members of my congregation became infected with the need to be more and more critical of my sermons and ministry. The good folks of this East Texas congregation were just itching for me to say something "unorthodox." I must have, yet I don't recall what I said. All I know is that in the weeks that followed more than one person asked me if I "believed in Jesus." This perplexed me. After all, I had devoted my entire life to the church, which in my mind suggests that Jesus is my "go-to guy," "wingman," and "copilot," to name just a few roles Jesus had played in my life. Jesus is also my "designated hitter," "the bomb," and "the captain of my ship." (If the thought of Jesus as my "wingman" upsets you, just know that the best pickup line in a Christian nightclub is "Jesus is my wingman.") Apparently I had said something—*something*—in one of my sermons that perked up at least one person's ears and, via telephone and parking lot conversations, spread to someone else's ears, and before I knew it I was no longer a *Christian*.

Whether I said something slightly askew or not, the truth is that I have always questioned the divinity of Jesus for precisely one reason: *I have no idea what that means.* To call Jesus "divine" is about as meaningful to me as calling Paula Dean's fried chicken "divine" (before she became an out-of-the-closet racist). I don't say this in order to demean Jesus. I say this because, again, I don't really know how to define divinity. Curiously, the dictionary defines divinity as "the quality or state of being divine," which is like saying a good person is a person who is good. To clarify, the dictionary links divinity with a god or goddess, which is about as helpful as saying a good person is a special kind of person who is good. But then there is my favorite entry in the dictionary's definition of "divine": "fudge made of whipped egg whites, sugar, and nuts." Well, there you have it. Jesus is like a dessert. This is why I like to add "causes diabetes" when my Pentecostal friends enthusiastically say, "Sweet Jesus!"

The view that Jesus is divine is not going away any time soon. It has been around since the New Testament started hinting that Jesus was no ordinary human being. John's Gospel is so enamored with Jesus that he makes what is perhaps the boldest claim about a man in the history of the written word: "In the beginning was the Word and the Word was with God and the Word was God. The Word was with God in the beginning. Everything came into being through the Word, and without the Word nothing came into being. What came into being through the Word was life, and the life was the light for all people. The light shines in the darkness, and the darkness doesn't extinguish the light."[25] In case the reader doesn't quite understand John's intent, he spells it out in splendid subtlety in verse 1:14: "The Word became flesh and made his home among us. We have seen his glory, glory like that of a father's only son, full of grace and truth." It's almost as if John is reading Matthew and Luke's account of the Virgin Birth and thinking, "Shoot, that ain't nothin'." Jesus wasn't just born into the world through one of the most common ways the VIPs of the ancient world were born—through the vaginal canal of a virgin. This is John's opportunity to one-up those who tried to lay claim to divinity, so he places Jesus at the very *beginning* of time. From a modern scientific perspective, Jesus was the dude that ignited the fireworks known as the "Big Bang." By the way, Jesus' relationship to science can be seen most clearly in the hit sitcom *The Big Bang Theory*. In the episode titled "The Luminous Fish Effect," Mary Cooper says about her son, Sheldon, "He gets his temper from his daddy. He's got my eyes. All that science stuff? Oh, that comes from Jesus."

Because of the developing tradition of Jesus' divinity, several new and interesting concepts entered the lexicon of the Christian faith, including the doctrine of the incarnation. John's assertion that in Jesus "the Word became flesh" is one way to understand his supposed divinity. We refer to this as "incarnation," a word that refers to the embodiment of divinity. As the *Son* of God, the same divinity that dwells in God also dwelled in Jesus. (Which leads me to ask, "If Jesus is God's Son, does that mean he was a twinkle in God's eye?") John's Gospel gets a lot of mileage out of the divinity/incarnation theme. Throughout his Gospel Jesus and God are linked together tighter than a _____. I couldn't think of anything that tight, so I'll let you fill in the blank. "Tighter than a fat guy in spandex" just seems so irreverent and politically incorrect. "The Father and I are one" pretty much sums up how tight they are.[26] John also makes hay with the "I am" statements, such as "I am the way," which does a not-so-subtle job of linking Jesus to the God of the Old Testament. I forgot to mention this earlier, and I'm not inclined to go back and find where it belongs: The overarching theme of the Old Testament is, "My god can kick your god's butt." Once you

25. John 1:1–5 (CEB).
26. John 10:30 (NRSV).

apply this hermeneutical (interpretive) lens to the Bible, you can kick butt in a Sunday school class discussion.

In the ensuing centuries the debate about Jesus' identity was the hottest topic around. Can you imagine how obsessed Fox News would have been about it, especially if someone would have suggested Jesus was a Muslim from Kenya? Everyone except the cashier at the 7-Eleven in Topeka, Kansas, was focused on Christology. The issue was debated at the first *seven* ecumenical councils. In fact, the ensuing debate about this book will probably lead to a worldwide ecumenical council too, as well as my excommunication from Christianity and a stockpiling of Hot Pockets as good-hearted folks prepare for Jesus' second coming. As I noted earlier, the Council of Chalcedon in 451 C.E. came to the mind-numbing conclusion that Jesus Christ consisted of both a human and a divine nature, "united with neither confusion nor division." (I look forward to learning that Jesus' divine atoms challenged his human atoms to a subatomic game of three-on-three basketball. A team consisting of a divine proton, neutron, and electron took on their human counterparts. It really wasn't a fair match. Some scientists believe this game inspired the modern-day games between the Harlem Globetrotters and Washington Generals.) The centuries went on and a lot of people attempted to tweak the doctrine of the incarnation of Christ. (This is not a reference to smoking meth.) For example, Thomas Aquinas, the father of modern Catholic theology, went so far as to suggest that even Jesus' *human* attributes were "perfect," which pretty much elevates the historical Jesus above any hint of humanity. Incarnation, in other words, creates a really Big Jesus! Thomas is also known as the founder of "Thomism." Seriously? When they put an "-ism" after your name and call it a movement you know you have stirred up some kick-ass karma.

The debate about the divinity of Jesus got so serious, in fact, that it confused many people and caused plenty of division. One of the most interesting doctrines that crawled out of the murky waters of Christology was called "Docetism." This comes from a Greek word that means "to seem," "apparition," or "phantom." Docetism argues that Jesus only seemed to be human; his physical body was a mere illusion. This effectively denied his humanity. The controversy over Docetism didn't last long, relatively speaking. It was rejected outright at the First Council of Nicaea in 325 C.E. The church regards it as heretical. Therefore, whatever we mean when we say Jesus was perfect in both divinity and humanity, we may not intellectually understand what divinity means, yet we sure as hell have a pretty good idea what humanity is all about. Even if we want to elevate his humanity to a state of perfection, we still want him to be one of us. For the record, I have yet to understand what a perfect human would be like. I suppose he or she would never lose a match on *Jeopardy* or have trouble with hemorrhoids. Any thoughts?

The christological craze didn't stop there. The renowned and oft-renounced John Shelby Spong writes, "As theology developed in the West, Jesus became first the divine Son of God, then the incarnation of the holy God, and finally the second person of the eternal Trinity of three persons in one God."[27] Ah, the Trinity. There's nothing more challenging than coming up with a children's sermon on Trinity Sunday every year to help "explain" the Trinity to a group of children *who could give a shit*. But hey, if you're going to make Jesus divine you have to find some way to explain God in heaven, God on earth and . . . God in between? The latter, of course, is my paean to the Holy Spirit, that mysterious go-between who comes dangerously close to being an "apparition" or "phantom." That's why the Pentecostals down the street keep referring to the Holy *Ghost*.

In my humble opinion, trying to explain Jesus' divinity and perfect humanity is difficult enough, and yet the church decided to exacerbate the situation by formulating the doctrine of the Trinity. Trinitarian theology is fun, of course, and allows a lot of room for creativity. Who hasn't heard the "liquid, ice, and vapor" analogy? This is the heresy of "modalism." Go ahead and use it. No one will notice. We could easily disregard the Trinity if it weren't for the fact that most Christians use the Trinitarian formula during the sacrament of baptism. Typically, we baptize folks "in the name of the Father, Son, and Holy Spirit." Clergy who are fed up with in-your-face patriarchal language, however, might use the phrase, "Creator, Redeemer, and Sustainer," which sounds more like a Viagra commercial than the formulation of a holy doctrine. In the meantime, we continue to confuse, if not piss off, our monotheistic siblings—Jews and Muslims—by giving them the impression that we worship *three gods*. We don't, of course (or maybe we do), yet you can't blame them for thinking this. We often sound "tri-theistic."

One of my church history professors at Hardin-Simmons University told us, "Every attempt in history to explain the Trinity has been labeled a

27. Spong, *New Christianity for a New World*, 111. Lloyd Geering similarly argues that the stages through which Jesus has progressed in Christian thought are as follows: Messiah (Christ), a Son of God, Lord, Savior, the only Son of God, the Logos or Word of God and creator of the world, the incarnation of God, and finally the second person of the Holy Trinity. Geering, *Christianity Without God*, 86.

heresy at one time or another." In other words, we are screwed if we even open our mouths. If committing the sin of heresy leads to eternal damnation then it might behoove us to stop trying to explain the Trinity, which means getting rid of it, which means demoting Jesus to his proper role as a human being, which means we should stop confusing people with references to God and the Holy Spirit as if they are somehow *different*. Let's be honest. The Holy Spirit has already been demoted to that mysterious force that teaches willing participants how to speak in tongues (i.e., glossolalia). The Holy Spirit is also good at knocking people down to the floor after the evangelist has spoken in tongues and laid hands forcefully on the willing participant's forehead (i.e., "slain in the Spirit"). Occasionally, if the willing participant is really "open to the Spirit," a demon or two can be expelled from the willing participant's body. Pretty cool stuff.

Let's be honest about one more thing: We aren't getting rid of the doctrine of the Trinity, mainly because we are enamored with things that come in threes, such as the Three Stooges, the Three Musketeers, and *My Three Sons*, to name just three examples. (I would have added a fourth example but that would have spoiled the mood.) We are ostensibly stuck with a Jesus who is more divine than human (if human at all) and who has been elevated to the second "person" in the three-person formulation that is fundamental to the orthodox Christian understanding of God. In other words, Jesus is exactly who he would have become if Dr. Doofenshmirtz had used him to take over the world: *the Christinator*. And that, my friends, is a Big Jesus!

4

Badass Jesus

I can only think of one word nuanced and strong enough to describe the missing piece in pop-culture's picture of Jesus: bad-ass.[1]

We are the Borg. You will be assimilated. Resistance is futile.[2]

I Know a Badass When I See One

Although I'm not a badass and have never been mistaken for one, I have a few in my family. On my dad's side of the family is my cousin Buddy, an old bull rider who now works for a propane company in Texas, like Hank Hill in the animated television series *King of the Hill*. He is a larger-than-life character who used to spend summers with my family in Sterling City, a small West Texas town surrounded by cattle and sheep ranches and oil jacks. Now the town is surrounded by gazillions of wind turbines because, you know, West Texans are known for their staunch environmentalist stance on clean, sustainable energy.

As a boy, I idolized Buddy for his free spirit and seemingly unlimited boldness. He was also a really good ballplayer. My dad used to announce some of the teenage league baseball games and would introduce him by saying, "Now at the plate, Goldilocks"—a reference to his long blonde hair. Long hair on a boy was a rarity in our small town because the local school would not allow a boy's hair to touch his eyes, his ears, or his collar.

1. "Bad-Ass Jesus."
2. From *Star Trek: Voyager*.

I sincerely believe the principal's primary responsibility was to monitor the male students for violations of the hair code and the female students for violations of a dress code that would not allow a skirt above the knees. Seems like a good use of his education to me!

Buddy is the nicest guy you would ever want to meet. He's also a genuine badass. He coaxed me into smoking my first joint at the age of fifteen. He snuck out at night and went swimming in backyard pools without the owners' knowledge. He climbed the water tower on more than one occasion. He also loved to fight. I once witnessed him picking a fight with a man who was standing too long in front of the beer cooler at a convenience store.

On my mom's side of the family there is my late uncle David. He lived down the road in San Angelo, Texas, and his reputation permeated every square inch of that West Texas city. I lived there as a young man and knew that if I ever got into a predicament he would somehow serve as my rescuer. In those days I attended Angelo State University, but I dropped out after a couple of years due to my inability to choose a major and my excessive marijuana use. The two may have been related, but I don't remember much from those days.

One story about David will suffice. One night I was in a local rock and roll bar when a biker walked up and chastised me for taking pictures of him and his friends who were sitting at a table. He said, "Why don't you take a picture? It will last longer." I didn't even have a camera on me. As I continued to defend my innocence, only to be threatened more and more, I instinctively asked, "Do you know David Rushing?" He paused and answered, "Yeah, what about him?" I said, "He's my uncle." The biker then said, rather sheepishly, "Dude! Why don't you come and have a beer with us!" Bikers are a wimpy lot.

My family history is peppered with stories of badass men. I'm trying not to be sexist, although I'm having a difficult time coming up with stories of women in my family who fit this description. The women in my family all seem to be very nice. However, I should give an honorable mention to my maternal grandmother, who raised eight children by herself after her husband left, including the above-mentioned David Rushing. She was extremely self-reliant and tough as nails. I think she would probably agree with the old adage, "Women need men like fish need bicycles."

My dad and his two brothers spent their summers living with their grandparents and uncles in a poverty-stricken African-American neighborhood. (For some reason, this part of town was called "Colored Town." Funny, the houses seem kind of drab to me.) Their grandfather was a bootlegger and their uncle John was a junkman. Another uncle, Wilburn, once killed a man for trespassing on his property. Family lore tells me that my paternal great-great-grandfather settled in West Texas because he was running from the law.

On my mom's side there was her grandfather, Harvey, who killed a man for attacking one of his sons and spent several years in prison for it. Then there is my uncle Kenny, the former rattlesnake hunter. Kenny was a champion hunter one year back in the early 1990s and decided to retire from the business after he nearly died from a snakebite. Karma's a bitch.

I could go on and on telling stories about some of these colorful characters. My point is that I know a badass when I see one, and Jesus was a badass . . . although not quite in the same way. In my childhood and early adult years I only heard about Big Jesus, the one I described in the previous chapter, the Christ of faith, the Christinator. This is the image of Jesus that began to develop after his untimely and shameful death. The early Christians decided to put a spin on his life and death, turning him into something that I would describe as "post-human." What I will do in this chapter is bring Jesus' humanity back into focus. I will rely primarily on the works of a few of today's best scholars of the historical Jesus and conclude that the Jesus of history was not Big Jesus, but *Badass* Jesus, the Jesus I began to know primarily after I finished my formal education.

In chapter 2 I introduced the reader to the beginning of the academic side of my spiritual autobiography, noting how my study of the Old Testament, Christian ethics, and process theology comprised the first three legs of my Christian journey. In this chapter I will write about the fourth leg of my journey: historical Jesus studies. This part of my journey took place roughly between the mid-1990s and the early 2000s, although I continue to be a student of historical Jesus studies. If I may summarize the academic side of my spiritual autobiography so far, it looks like this:

1. Old Testament studies introduced me to a critical way of reading and utilizing the Bible.

2. Christian ethics helped me to develop a greater awareness of social justice issues.

3. Process theology gave me a theological framework that allows me to think about God.

4. Historical Jesus studies taught me how to understand Jesus in a way that makes him relevant for contemporary Christians.

All of these legs in my spiritual/academic autobiography have helped me in my preaching and teaching ministry as a pastor of local churches in the past two and a half decades, although I must admit that my ministry has not always been appreciated. To be blunt, some people think I suck as a pastor.

The goal of this chapter is to begin the process of offering a recultivation of the Jesus tradition, particularly in the manner in which we imagine Jesus. After all, even the work of historians is largely an imaginative process.[3] I choose the word "recultivate" because it is an agrarian term, and the Jesus movement was born in an agrarian culture. Notice the root word "cult" in the words "cultivation" and "culture." It is time to admit that almost everything about our lives, from our religious views to our outlook on life to our cultural existence, is "cultish." For over two thousand years, the church has been cultivating an image of Jesus that sometimes yields good fruit but often does not. To cultivate means:

1. To prepare and work on (land) in order to raise crops; till.

2. To promote or improve the growth of (a plant, crop, etc.) by labor and attention.[4]

In my opinion, and in the opinion of many of the historical Jesus scholars, it is time to recultivate Jesus' image, which in turn promises to recultivate Christianity. The "crops" we have raised in the past, tilled from the ground with the Christ of faith, have too often produced a brand of Christianity that is mired in rigid dogma, intolerant of other perspectives and lifestyles, and uses violence as a way to solve problems. I don't need to remind the reader of Christianity's sordid past. (The Crusades and the Inquisitions come to mind, as well as pedophile priests and slimy televangelists.) It's not just the past that is questionable, however. A 2007 study released by the Barna Group, a reputable evangelical research and polling firm, found that young adults are rejecting the church today because they perceive it to be too anti-gay, insensitive, judgmental, hypocritical, old-fashioned, and involved in politics.[5]

3. See Axtell, "History as Imagination."

4. "Cultivate," Dictionary.com, online: http://dictionary.reference.com/browse/cultivate?s=t.

5. Kinnaman and Lyons, *Unchristian*, 34.

The connection between the Christ of faith and the negative aspects of the Christian faith are not readily apparent, and yet it seems to me that if the central figure of a religion is imbued with all kinds of fantastic and incredulous powers, then the followers of that figure will try their best to maintain that power through preaching, teaching, and institutional control. In other words, Big Jesus has produced Big Christianity, a Christianity that has no problem wielding its power with the sword as well as the sacraments. The sacraments have been the central focus of many of the disputes between Jesus' followers. To give one example, the church has often used the Lord's Table (i.e., Communion or Eucharist) to control who gets to receive God's grace and who doesn't. In my view, everyone should be invited to the Lord's Table. The only criteria for receiving the Eucharist should be whether someone is physically or spiritually hungry.

What is needed in Christianity is not Big Jesus, but Badass Jesus. By that, I don't mean a Jesus who enjoys picking a fight in front of a beer cooler, but a Jesus who is so bad he doesn't *need* to fight—ditto for his followers. (I don't mean "bad" in a moral sense, but "bad" in the pop culture way of saying someone is really awesome. Sort of like Tom Petty and the Heartbreakers.) In this chapter we will briefly discuss some of the badass qualities of the historical Jesus through the writings of some of the biggest names today in historical Jesus studies. This is a Jesus that is more political than theological, although there are many theological implications.

The Day I Got to Be a Fellow

In 1999 I was called to a Christian Church, Disciples of Christ (DOC) congregation in Big Spring, Texas. (When I say "called" I don't mean I literally heard God speaking to me. God only speaks to a small fraction of mentally ill people who aren't medicated sufficiently with a pill called "the God Silencer." The rest of us just have to guess what God might be saying to us.) Because I was largely unfamiliar with the DOC I began reading about them and was particularly fascinated with their historical connection to the Stone-Campbell Movement or "Restoration Movement" of the early nineteenth century. I encourage you to read about Alexander Campbell, Barton Stone, and the other founders of this unique American Christian movement. The Disciples of Christ, Churches of Christ, and the Independent Christian Churches all trace their roots to this early nineteenth-century movement. (Too bad they don't like each other very much.) This movement sought to *restore* Christianity to its apostolic roots. They wanted the modern church to pattern itself after the church we observe in the New Testament. This was easier said than done, because even in the New Testament we find factions and disputes about orthodoxy (right belief) and orthopraxis (right practice). For example, some people drove camels and some preferred donkeys. Donkey riders liked to put rear-end stickers on their animals showing a donkey pissing on a camel. Well, that's not true. Or maybe it was. I have no idea.

At the time of my calling to this congregation, I was fully immersed in historical Jesus studies, particularly the works produced by members of the Jesus Seminar. As I noted earlier, these guys (and a few women) are called "Jesus Fellows." One day I was reading about Robert Funk, the founder of the Jesus Seminar, and I learned that he began his career as a DOC minister. Immediately I made the connection in my mind between the Restoration Movement in DOC history and the Jesus Seminar's quest to discover the authentic voice of Jesus. This was the Seminar's project in the 1980s and 1990s. (Since then they have moved on to other worthwhile projects, such as trying to figure out how stoned the writer of the book of Revelation was, especially when he wrote chapter 4.)

They pursued the authentic voice of Jesus through independent research and annual meetings at the Seminar in Santa Rosa, California. There they discussed, debated, and voted on the words attributed to Jesus in the Gospels. Their voting system is highly sophisticated. They use colored beads. Red means, "Yea, Jesus said that." Pink means, "He probably said something very similar to that." Gray means, "I don't think so, buster." And black means, "Speak to the hand because the face don't understand." Or something like that. They concluded that only a small fraction of the words attributed to Jesus in the Gospels are authentically the voice of Jesus. This compelled me to preach a sermon titled "Less Is More," which you can read at the end of this chapter. The point of my sermon is that if we Christians try to follow only the passages in the Gospels the Jesus Seminar deems authentic we will be less bogged down in all the other crap in the Bible, such as trying to interpret the fourth chapter of the book of Revelation.

From my perspective, the goals of the Restoration Movement of the early nineteenth century and the Jesus Seminar of the late twentieth century are very similar. While the Restoration Movement sought to restore Christianity to its New Testament roots, the Jesus Seminar sought to restore Christianity to its *Gospel* roots. The Jesus Seminar is not the first attempt to try to understand who the historical Jesus really was. Albert Schweitzer summarized previous attempts in his highly acclaimed but criticized 1906 book, *The Quest of the Historical Jesus*. The second quest took place in the mid-twentieth century with the likes of John A. T. Robinson's *A New Quest of the Historical Jesus*. I don't have the space or desire to summarize the findings of the second quest, although the fact that a third quest arose in the 1980s suggests that it didn't quite do the job.[6]

I emailed Robert Funk and asked him if his DOC background had anything to do with his founding of the Jesus Seminar. He acknowledged that he had never consciously thought of the connection between Restorationism and the Jesus Seminar; still, he was intrigued by the possibility. More importantly, he invited me to the next Jesus Seminar! I decided to go and was astonished to discover that they had made a place for me *at the table*. They use a large horseshoe table configuration for their deliberations. They are also surrounded by an audience of curious onlookers who wish they could play with those colored beads. I never went back to the Seminar, primarily because I couldn't afford it, and yet I will never forget the time I got to be a "Fellow."

Generally speaking, what were the conclusions of the Jesus Seminar? One of the *real* Jesus Fellows, Charles Hedrick, offers the following "Premises" of the work of the Jesus Seminar, which I find very helpful. Don't read this if you have a weak stomach or a strong evangelical background. Note the added sarcasm in italics:

1. The early Christian gospels, both canonical and non-canonical, are theological interpretations of Jesus. Hence, all information they contain serves the interest of early Christian faith in some way. "Canonical" refers to those books in the Bible the early church decided are of "divine inspiration." *Catholics and Protestants disagree about which books are canonical, which I think is a good reason to kill one another.*

2. Early Christian literature contains no verbatim sayings of Jesus. What is attributed to him was given its present form in the early Christian movement, both in the oral period and later when the traditions had been reduced to writing.

3. Thus, the words attributed to Jesus in early Christian literature are the words of early Christian faith, and their description of his activities

6. For a good summary of all three quests for the historical Jesus, see Bessler, *Scandalous Jesus*.

constitutes the early Christian view of how the Christ ought to have comported himself. *I think it's awesome that Jesus could comport himself!*

4. We may hope to hear an echo of the voice of the historical man, and sketch in barest outline some details of his life.

5. The criterion of dissimilarity/distinctiveness is the most reliable tool in the search for the words of the historical man. *In other words, if it sounds a little crazy, Jesus probably said it.*

6. The findings of the Jesus Seminar constitute an irreducible minimum of the historical data.

7. It is not possible to know what Jesus thought of himself. *Although we are pretty sure he had really good self-esteem. He may have even had a messiah complex.*

8. Inferences may be drawn from the historical data. An inference is a reader's interpretation of data and should not be confused with the data itself.

9. The same data will allow different inferences.

10. A reconstructed Jesus is not Jesus as he actually was, but Jesus at his most radical dimensions (i.e., Badass Jesus). The reconstruction, if it is reliably done, has eliminated much of what Jesus had in common with first-century Palestinian Judaism and earliest Christianity.

11. Thus, we can hope to see the historical man only in his most radical dimensions.

12. Responsible profiles are always "under construction." By its very nature, the data and our critical methodologies will not allow a final definitive view of Jesus.[7]

Despite my attempts at humor and sarcasm, and despite the fact that the historical Jesus is not easily discernible, I will attempt to present a profile of Jesus with as much integrity as possible. I understand that not everyone will receive this book with as much glee as I have had in writing it because, similar to the way many Christians see the Jesus Seminar, I am in danger of becoming "the Grinch who stole Christmas."[8]

7. Hedrick, "Jesus of Nazareth," in Hoover, ed., *Profiles of Jesus*, 65–66.

8. Hedrick, "The 'Good News' about the Historical Jesus," in Bessler-Northcutt et al., *Historical Jesus Goes to Church*, 91.

Play that Funky Music

In one of his latest books, former megachurch pastor and author Rob Bell talks about what he felt was so unique about Alcoholics Anonymous meetings as he began attending them in response to a parishioner's request. He writes, "Slowly it dawned on me what it was: I was in a bullshit-free zone."[9] Bell is also known for using the word "bullshit" on a Christian radio program in 2013 as he was being unnecessarily provoked for his increasingly progressive views on homosexuality. For some reason, many evangelical Christians are fixated on homosexuality because, you know, heterosexuals can't follow Jesus with all those rainbow flags out there.

The phrase "bullshit-free zone" is an accurate way to describe my reaction to historical Jesus studies as well. There is little or no effort to bullshit Jesus into some kind of theological straightjacket. The historical Jesus is the man we would observe if we had the ability to follow him around with our smart phones or cameras. We might see Jesus teaching and consoling and throwing fits in temples, but we would not see him as the Messiah, Son of God, or Lord and savior. These are theological constructs applied to Jesus by sincere but overly eager Christians. The purpose of this book, in contrast, is to give the reader—Christian or otherwise—a little breathing room from the forced piety and orthodoxy of Sunday morning worship, radio and television evangelists, feel-good fluffy Christian literature, and apocalyptic street preachers. So now that we are in an established bullshit-free zone, what can we say with at least a modicum of confidence about the historical Jesus? By the way, this book's bullshit-free zone should not be confused with Fox News cult personality Bill O'Reilly's "No Spin Zone," which spins so hard I can feel the hot air blowing out of my television set.

A good place to start is with the late founder of the Jesus Seminar, Robert "Play that Funky Music" Funk. This is the name ESPN cult personality Chris Berman would have given Dr. Funk if the latter had been a ballplayer. Funk was convinced that the Jesus Seminar had laid the foundation for a new Reformation. "Christianity as we have known it is anemic and wasting away," he says. "It is time to reinvent Christianity, complete with new symbols, new stories, and a new understanding of Jesus."[10] Funk tries to do just that. Like a singer—funky music or otherwise—Funk believes Jesus left us a *voiceprint*. Beginning with the premise that Jesus was "a wan-

9. Bell, *What We Talk About*, 138.

10. Powell, *Jesus as a Figure in History*, 73.

dering teacher of wisdom," Funk argues that Jesus' voiceprint is found in the Gospels primarily through his aphorisms, parables, and dialogues.[11] An aphorism is a short, pithy witticism (such as, "A penny for your thoughts 'cause they ain't worth a nickel," which is *my* witticism, by the way). In these sayings, and in his actions, "we can occasionally catch sight of Jesus' vision of God's domain."[12] Through his meticulous study of the words and actions of Jesus, Funk offers seven insights into the historical Jesus. Any hint of sarcasm, written in italics, is my gift to the discussion:

1. Jesus was a sage. Here he belongs to the wisdom tradition of ancient Israel, which is *not* concerned with theories of sin and salvation, but how to cope with life.

2. Jesus was an exorcist. Even though we don't believe in the existence of demons today, people in that time and place did, and *Jesus was the Prozac of his day.*

3. Jesus advocated a trust ethic. He admonished his followers not to worry about such things as food, clothing, and shelter. *I hope he was exaggerating.*

4. Jesus believed in a God who treats all human beings evenhandedly. As Funk describes it, "Kinship in the kingdom means dwelling in a house without walls." *Except bathroom walls. We have to have bathroom walls.*

5. Jesus was always in a celebratory mood. Celebration is a thread that runs all throughout his stories and short sayings. *In contemporary terms, we would call Jesus a "party animal" in the mode of a John Belushi—a much thinner (and shorter) John Belushi.*

6. Jesus had a wicked sense of humor. This contrasts with a moralistic Jesus, which is the way many contemporary conservative Christians imagine him to have been. *For many Christians today, Jesus was moralistically against such things as cussing, smoking, drugs, abortions, birth control, premarital sex, homosexual sex, rock and roll music, environmentalists, Democrats, gun haters, pacifists, illegal immigrants, MSNBC, witchcraft, and reading Harry Potter books. In reality, the only thing Jesus was against was religious nuts.*

11. Funk, *Credible Jesus*, 2.
12. Funk, in Jesus Seminar, *Once and Future Jesus*, 15.

7. Jesus died on a cross. This is because he was unwilling to compromise his integrity and his vision of the kingdom of God.[13]

My intent is not to inundate the reader with lists, however Funk ends his book *Honest to Jesus* with a really great summary of what our "thirst to know the flesh-and-blood Jesus" means for contemporary Christians. My hope is that this list with provoke further interest in Funk and the Jesus Seminar's work on the historical Jesus. I offer this list, of course, with a few added notes of sarcasm (in italics):

1. The aim of the quest (for the historical Jesus) is to set Jesus free "from the scriptural and creedal and experiential prisons in which we have incarcerated him."

2. The quest prompts us to revamp our understanding of the origins of the Christian faith itself.

3. The quest also has serious ramifications for how we understand the Christian life.

4. The quest points to a secular sage who may have more relevance to the spiritual dimensions of society at large than to institutionalized religion.

5. We can no longer rest our faith on the faith of Peter or the faith of Paul.

6. Jesus himself is not the proper object of faith. *This is especially true in rural America, where guns are the proper object of faith.*

7. In articulating the vision of Jesus, we should take care to express our interpretations in the same register as he employed in his parables and aphorisms. In other words, we should keep our vision of Jesus open-ended. *Nothing is chiseled in stone . . . except the dates on our tombstones.*

8. Give Jesus a demotion. *That's sort of what this book is about; however, I have not given him a pay cut!*

9. We need to cast Jesus in a new drama, assign him a role in a story with a different plot. *We could always create a new* Law and Order *and cast him as a defense attorney for cheating tax collectors and homely hookers.*

13. Ibid, 15–19.

10. We need to reconceive the vocation of Jesus as the Christ. *Being a "Christ" is a pretty cool job. I'm looking for one on Craigslist.*

11. Jesus kept an open table. *Can I just go on record to say that a denomination or congregation that does not practice an open table is not a real church? If that pisses anyone off then I suggest you open up your damn table.*

12. Jesus made forgiveness reciprocal, *which is being tit for tat in a nice way.*

13. Jesus condemned the public practice of piety. *Can we not stop with the annoying prayers in restaurants for goodness' sake? Are we really afraid we will get food poisoning if we don't bless the meal?*

14. Jesus advocated an unbrokered relationship with God, *which means he cut out the middleman.*

15. Jesus robs his followers of Christian "privilege."

16. Jesus makes it clear that all rewards and punishments are intrinsic.

17. We will have to abandon the doctrine of the blood atonement. *I can just hear some Christians saying, "Well, then, how am I gonna get saved?"*

18. We will need to interpret the reports of the resurrection for what they are: our glimpse of what Jesus glimpsed.

19. Redeem sex, and Mary, Jesus' mother, by restoring to Jesus a biological if not actual father. *In other words, stop with the "divine adultery" theory. God is tired of being red-faced.*

20. Exorcise the apocalyptic elements from Christianity. *I guess this means Tim LaHaye needs an exorcism. Ironic, eh?*

21. Declare the New Testament a highly uneven and biased record of various early attempts to invent Christianity. *As an aside, have you ever wondered what the Bible would look like if it had been written today with computer and Internet technology? For starters, all the biblical authors would have a really cool Facebook page.*

Funk concludes his book with this sentence: "These are my twenty-one theses. If I had a church, I would scotch tape them to the door." Unlike Martin Luther, Funk apparently never learned how to use a hammer.[14]

14. Funk, *Honest to Jesus*, 300–314.

Sponge Bob Square Pants

Funk is not the only contemporary scholar who has called for a new Reformation, primarily in the way we understand Jesus. The retired American Episcopalian bishop John Shelby "Sponge Bob Square Pants" Spong has made his name almost synonymous with the word "controversial" through his writings, including *Rescuing the Bible from Fundamentalism* (1991), *Why Christianity Must Change or Die* (1998), and *A New Christianity for a New World* (2001). In these books and others he criticizes the core theological perspective of traditional Christianity, called "theism." In classical theism, God is personal and present and active in the way the world and universe is governed and organized. Spong does not believe theism is a credible and valid conception of God, and many Christians agree with him. He suggests there are many "believers in exile" today because people are naturally incredulous of the more incredible claims of the Christian faith. He famously refers to those who have given up on the church as the "Church Alumni Association." Therefore, he believes many of the church's traditional doctrines should be reformulated or, as I prefer to call it, "recultivated." As Spong argues, "Sometimes the dead wood of the past must be cleared out so that new life has a chance to grow."[15] He is referring specifically to the image of Jesus as a "divine rescuer." Who hasn't heard the following words from a preacher?: "Jesus died for my sins. He shed his precious blood on the cross of Calvary for my salvation. I have been washed in the blood of the lamb. Through the sacrifice of Jesus, I have been saved. The stain of sin on my soul has been cleansed." (Just for kicks, I once took a bath in lamb blood. It didn't do me a damn bit of good, but the lamb chops were awesome.)

Spong hasn't given up on Jesus, however. In his writings he expresses great love and admiration for the man from Galilee. He calls Jesus the "central figure" of his faith story.[16] He states that he is a Christian because he believes that Jesus Christ fully expressed the presence of a God of compassion and selfless love, and that this is the meaning of the early Christian proclamation, "Jesus is Lord."[17] Still, he rejects traditional doctrines such as Jesus' divinity, virgin birth, and physical resurrection, leaving people wondering just what Spong still finds attractive about Jesus. In a chapter titled, "Jesus Beyond Incarnation," Spong claims he sees a "new portrait

15. Spong, *Why Christianity Must Change or Die*, 83.
16. Spong, *New Christianity for a New World*, 130.
17. "John Shelby Spong."

of Jesus," a Jesus who was more deeply and fully alive than anyone else. Jesus pointed to something he called the realm (or kingdom) of God, where new possibilities demand to be considered. Finally, Jesus was constantly dismantling barriers that separate people from one another, including barriers caused by tribal fears, human prejudice, gender and sexual distinctions, and religious differences.[18] (I'm still not in favor of breaking down bathroom walls, however. I need my space.)

In his book *Why Christianity Must Change or Die*, Spong distinguishes between "Jesus the Rescuer" and "Christ the Spirit Person."[19] The Rescuer, of course, is rooted in the doctrine of the atonement, which teaches that Jesus rescued us from our sins by dying on the cross. Obviously, this poses a lot of theological problems, such as the notion of a bloodthirsty god. On the other hand, Spong notes that from the very beginning of the Christian experience the word "spirit" was used in reference to Jesus. "Spirit" is a difficult word to define, yet it allows room for our imaginations about the historical Jesus to come out and play. Interestingly, Spong uses the name "Jesus" in connection with the "Rescuer" image, and "Christ" in reference to the "Spirit Person." I would prefer to flip those terms and talk about "Jesus the Spirit Person" and "Christ the Rescuer" because the Spirit Person is a historically imagined figure whereas the Rescuer is a faith-imagined figure.

In the tradition of Martin Luther and the above-mentioned Robert Funk, Spong also sought to communicate his "Call for Reformation." His controversial but celebrated twelve theses are as follows (again, with added sarcasm in italics):

1. Theism, as a way of defining God, is dead. So most theological God-talk is today meaningless. A new way to speak of God must be found.

2. Since God can no longer be conceived in theistic terms, it becomes nonsensical to seek to understand Jesus as the incarnation of the theistic deity. So the Christology of the ages is bankrupt. *Bankrupt? I don't know . . . the televangelists still make a boatload of money on Big Jesus . . . although I hear Robert Schuller's Crystal Cathedral went belly-up.*

18. Spong, *New Christianity for a New World*, 131–37; *Jesus for the Non-Religious*, part 3.

19. Spong, *Why Christianity Must Change or Die*, chs. 6, 7.

3. The biblical story of the perfect and finished creation from which human beings fell into sin is pre-Darwinian mythology and post-Darwinian nonsense. *May I theorize for a moment? I prefer to think that "sin" entered the world the first time a caveman hit his cavewoman on the head with a large stick and the following thought entered his head: "I shouldn't have done that. She might hit me back."*

4. The virgin birth, understood as literal biology, makes Christ's divinity, as traditionally understood, impossible. *Unless you buy into the theory that virgins can get pregnant in a bathtub. Wait, did they have bathtubs back then?*

5. The miracle stories of the New Testament can no longer be interpreted in a post-Newtonian world as supernatural events performed by an incarnate deity.

6. The view of the cross as the sacrifice for the sins of the world is a barbarian idea based on primitive concepts of God and must be dismissed. *Okay, let's get down to brass tacks. This is absolutely the stupidest doctrine in Christianity and seemingly the most ubiquitous. That's it. I'm done speaking about it. If anyone still believes in "sacrificial atonement" they should lose their voting rights.*

7. Resurrection is an action of God. Jesus was raised into the meaning of God. It therefore cannot be a physical resuscitation occurring inside human history. *Spong loses me here when he says, "Jesus was raised into the meaning of God." I think he was afraid he would permanently lose his bishop hat if he protested the resurrection too much.*[20]

8. The story of the ascension assumes a three-tiered universe and is therefore not capable of being translated into the concepts of a post-Copernican space age. *The story of the ascension would be more believable if Jesus had put on an astronaut's uniform; yet how freaky would it be to read the words "astronaut's uniform" in a two-thousand-year-old book?*

9. There is no external, objective, revealed standard written in scripture or on tablets of stone that will govern our ethical behavior for all time.

10. Prayer cannot be a request made to a theistic deity to act in human history in a particular way.

20. Spong more fully attempts to explain the resurrection of Jesus in his book, *Resurrection: Myth or Reality?*

11. The hope for life after death must be separated forever from the behavior control mentality of reward and punishment. The church must abandon, therefore, its reliance on guilt as a motivator of behavior.

12. All human beings bear God's image and must be respected for what each person is. Therefore, no external description of one's being, whether based on race, ethnicity, gender, or sexual orientation, can properly be used as the basis for either rejection or discrimination.[21] *Although if it were up to me—and it's not—I would discriminate based on political orientation. It's time to separate the sheep from the goats!*

Spong definitely has a way of stirring up the proverbial pot—or just a regular pot, I'm sure. In fact, I hear he cooks a mean stew . . . The bottom line is that Spong's Jesus is, shall we say, much more "muscular" than the Jesus we hear about on television and cheesy YouTube videos. Spong's Jesus is kind of a badass.

Don't Double-Cross Me

Perhaps the most passionate purveyor of the Badass Jesus is the Irish-American New Testament scholar and former Catholic priest John Dominic "Don't Double-Cross Me" Crossan, one of the foremost historical Jesus scholars in the world and a cofounder of the Jesus Seminar. Crossan's books are muscular in tone, with such titles as *Jesus: A Revolutionary Biography*; *The Historical Jesus: The Life of a Mediterranean Jewish Peasant*; and *God and Empire: Jesus against Rome, Then and Now*. Like an Irish street fighter, Crossan has proposed some theories about the historical Jesus that would land any soft-jawed fundamentalist on his or her arse.

In his tome *The Historical Jesus*, Crossan argues that Jesus can only be understood within the context of first-century Judaism, although Judaism then was as diverse as it is now. Rather than understand Jesus as a trained rabbi, as others have done, Crossan suggests Jesus was a peasant Jewish Cynic, one who had "a way of looking and dressing, of eating, living, and relating that announced its contempt for honor and shame, for patronage and clientage."[22] The following is a nice summary statement of Crossan's view of Jesus as a peasant Jewish Cynic:

21. "A New Christianity for a New World."

22. Crossan, *Historical Jesus*, 421. For the argument that Jesus can only be understood within the context of first-century Judaism, see Sanders, *Jesus and Judaism*. Sander's

His strategy, implicitly for himself and explicitly for his followers, was the combination of *free healing and common eating*, a religious and economic egalitarianism that negated alike and at once the hierarchical and patronal normalcies of Jewish religion and Roman power. And, lest he himself be interpreted as simply the new broker of a new God, he moved on constantly, settling down neither at Nazareth nor Capernaum. He was neither broker nor mediator but, somewhat paradoxically, the announcer that neither should exist between humanity and divinity or humanity and itself.[23]

As a cofounder of the Jewish Seminar, most of his conclusions sound very, shall we say, Seminar-ish. He is critical, of course, of the miraculous claims of the Gospels, asserting instead that Jesus was known early on as a powerful magician, which is just another way of saying he was known for his healing powers. Perhaps Jesus was a first-century David Copperfield in that he was very good at tricks such as pulling a camel through the eye of a needle. Or perhaps not. Crossan argues that the Gospel writers never intended for their works to be taken literally. The *meaning* of a story or parable is important, not its historical veracity. For example, the meaning of the resurrection is more important than the *mode*, such as whether we should take the account literally or metaphorically.[24] Crossan is also the scholar who famously argued that Jesus' body was devoured by wild animals rather than placed in a tomb. If such an argument ever turned out to be true it would really screw up all those Passion plays!

Although Crossan refers to Jesus as "revolutionary," he was nonviolent. The titles the early Christians applied to Jesus such as "Son of God," "Lord," and "Savior" were also titles applied to Caesar Augustus before Jesus was even born. To say "Jesus is Lord," therefore, means Caesar is *not* Lord. Crossan writes, "They [the Christians] were taking the identity of the Roman emperor and giving it to a Jewish peasant. Either that was a peculiar joke and a very low lampoon, or it was what the Romans called *majestas* and

---

Jesus contrasts with Crossan's in that Jesus is not a wandering cynic philosopher but, like Schweitzer argued, an eschatological prophet. The latter is a Jesus who unfortunately was wrong because the world didn't come to an end. To better appreciate a Jewish Jesus and the possibility of interfaith dialogue between Christians and Jews, read Levine, *The Misunderstood Jew*. For an emphasis on Jesus as rabbi, see Chilton, *Rabbi Jesus*.

23. Crossan, *Historical Jesus*, 422. Italics are his, although Crossan borrowed the whole concept of italics from other great writers.

24. Crossan and Wright, *Resurrection of Jesus*, 28–29.

we call high treason."[25] This implies that Jesus was not a *non-resister*; he was a practitioner of *nonviolent resistance*, as evidenced by the fact that he "announced and enacted the kingdom of God."[26] Speaking of the kingdom of God, one of my favorite Crossan quotes is: "The Kingdom of God is what the world would be if God were directly and immediately in charge."[27] Think about that for a moment. If God were directly in charge puppies would never die, the Taliban would be a kite-selling corporation, and Led Zeppelin would still be recording. Or at least I like to think so.

The full extent of Crossan's historical imagination is beyond the scope of this book, but one of the most important points he makes about Jesus is his practice of "open commensality." "Commensality" is derived from the Latin word *mensa*, meaning "table." According to Crossan, "It means the rules of tabling and eating as miniature models for the rules of association and socialization. It means table fellowship as a map of economic discrimination, social hierarchy, and political differentiation."[28] Jesus practiced and preached through his parables *open* commensality, that is, an open table. This explains why Jesus garnered a reputation as a glutton, a drunkard, and a friend of tax collectors and sinners. Because women were often present at his table—especially unmarried women—Jesus was accused of socializing with whores, which is one reason I have suggested that the parable of the prodigal son, which implies that the son wasted much of his inheritance on whores, is autobiographical.

Crossan's Jesus—heck, *our* Jesus—was a revolutionary egalitarian ba-dass. And the fact that Crossan is an ex-Catholic priest who believes in the open table should not be lost on the reader. This is a strong uppercut to his former church, which practices a closed table. Dumbasses.

Resistance Is Futile

Perhaps the most influential author in my spiritual-intellectual journey is Marcus "Resistance Is Futile" Borg, a Jesus Seminar Fellow and former professor at Oregon State University. Ever since Borg's breakout book, *Meeting Jesus Again for the First Time* (1994), he has had an enormous impact on liberal-progressive American Christianity and abroad. Much like the

25. Crossan, *God and Empire*, 28.

26. Crossan and Reed, *Excavating Jesus*, 214.

27. Crossan, *Jesus*, 55.

28. Ibid, 68.

"Borg" in a couple of the *Star Trek* television series, resistance to Borg's teachings about Jesus is *futile*. If anyone in this day and age wants to *assimilate* to the Christian faith, they must first work through the writings of Marcus Borg. Yes, I have a man crush on Marcus Borg.

Borg's understanding of Jesus begins with his distinction between the Jesus of history and the Christ of faith. He reformulates this distinction and uses the terms "pre-Easter Jesus" and "post-Easter Jesus." Pre-Easter Jesus is the man who lived between the years 4 B.C.E. and 30 C.E. He is a figure of the past, a corporeal (flesh and blood), finite, mortal human being. Like Crossan, Borg argues that Jesus of Nazareth was a Jewish peasant. The post-Easter Jesus, on the other hand, is the Jesus of tradition and experience. This is the Jesus portrayed in history after his death and proclaimed resurrection. He is a figure of the present rather than the past, a spiritual, nonmaterial being. He is infinite, eternal, and divine, the King of kings and Lord of lords. This is Jesus the Christ.[29] According to Borg, "the Gospels contain minimally two voices—the voice of the pre-Easter Jesus and the voice of the community in the post-Easter setting."[30] In most of Borg's writings, however, he focuses on the pre-Easter Jesus.

So, who was this pre-Easter Jesus anyway? Like many other contemporary Jesus scholars, Borg places Jesus within the context of Judaism, maintaining that Jesus never intended to establish a new religion. Jesus "saw himself as having a mission within Judaism."[31] He was trying to affect positive change within his inherited religion, using his many gifts and abilities. In his book *Meeting Jesus Again for the First Time*, Borg gives some impressions of Jesus, claiming Jesus had remarkable verbal skills, including his ability to tell stories and parables, offer short sayings, and engage in debate. Jesus was a master at using dramatic public actions, such as eating with sinners, entering Jerusalem on the back of a donkey, and overturning moneychangers' tables in the temple. There was a "radical social and political edge" to Jesus' message and activity. Furthermore, he was known as a healer. More healing stories are told about Jesus, Borg claims, "than about anybody else in the Jewish tradition." Finally, Jesus must have been a remarkable person because he lived such a brief life, but hey, we're still talking about him.[32]

29. Borg, ed., *Jesus at 2000*, 8.

30. Borg, *Meeting Jesus Again for the First Time*, 21.

31. Ibid, 22. Neither did Jesus see himself as the Messiah, a label that belongs to the post-Easter Jesus. See Borg and Wright, *Meaning of Jesus*, 53.

32. Ibid, 30–31.

In several of his writings, Borg offers a sketch of the historical Jesus, intentionally using non-messianic categories, but placing him squarely within the Jewish tradition of his time and place. Borg lays out this sketch in a way that only Borg can: with precision, clarity, and simplicity. The beauty of Borg is that his writings are accessible to almost everyone. My dog, Jake, however, had a difficult time trying to read Borg. Jake is more interested in *eating* Borg's books.

Borg paints a picture of Jesus using five broad strokes, beginning with the image of Jesus as a Jewish mystic:

> As foundational, my claim that Jesus was a Jewish mystic means Jesus was one for whom God was an experiential reality. He was one of those people for whom the sacred was, to use William James' terms, a firsthand religious experience rather than a secondhand belief. Mystics, as I use the term, are people who have decisive and typically frequent firsthand experiences of the sacred.[33]

Borg claims the Gospels point to Jesus' mystical experiences: "the language of 'Spirit,' the tradition that Jesus had visions, the reports of him engaging in long hours of prayer, and his healings."[34] He also refers to Jesus as a "Spirit person," which in his view is interchangeable with being a "mystic" or "ecstatic."[35] He claims that "the most crucial fact about Jesus was that he was a 'Spirit person,' a 'mediator of the sacred,' one of those persons in human history to whom the Spirit was an experiential reality."[36] Borg also lists other mystics of the Jewish tradition, including the patriarchs, Moses, Elijah, and the classical prophets.

He then builds upon his view that Jesus was a Jewish mystic—someone who had a firsthand experience with the divine—by painting a picture of him with four other specific brush strokes: Jesus was a healer, a wisdom teacher, a social prophet, and a movement founder. I'll discuss each one briefly.

Only a small percentage of mystics were healers, Borg claims, but Jesus seems to have been a member of this small minority. Here Borg may surprise modern readers of the Bible with his claim that "the gospel traditions about Jesus as healer and exorcist reflect historical happenings."[37] He does not believe Jesus performed any nature miracles (such as walking on water), but he

33. Ibid., 60.
34. Borg, in Hoover, ed., *Profiles of Jesus*, 132.
35. Borg and Wright, *Meaning of Jesus*, 60.
36. Borg, *Meeting Jesus Again for the First Time*, 31–32.
37. Borg, in Hoover, ed., *Profiles of Jesus*, 133.

does suggest that Jesus "effected healings" and performed what he and his contemporaries experienced as exorcisms. Borg is also careful to clarify the difference between "healing illness" (removing the social consequences of an illness such as leprosy) and "curing disease" (curing the organic condition itself). He argues that Jesus was able to do both, without explaining *how* Jesus was able to cure diseases.[38] Borg doesn't accept the supernatural interventionist model of God, and yet he also clearly states that we can't just reduce everything to "psychosomatic" healings either. My own take on this is that one or two "healings" in a place and time with very little medical knowledge could go a long way to excite the general public and gain a huge following. In the ancient world, people were desperate for a healer.

It was his reputation as a healer and exorcist that helped him draw crowds for his teaching moments. The Jewish peasants may not have been as desperate for wisdom teachers or sages as they were for healers, yet they were certainly drawn toward people who could articulate an alternative vision of the world. Like illiterate people today, the Jewish peasants in first-century Palestine could care less about the intelligentsia, but they obviously listened to someone who was subversive toward the elites. The irony is that Jesus' teachings are subversive toward *everyone*. According to Borg, Jesus stood out among other sages of his day because his wisdom was so subversive. Wisdom comes in two forms, says Borg: conventional and unconventional (subversive, alternative). Jesus challenged the conventional wisdom of his world (and ours as well). Borg writes, "Like Socrates, Jesus was a teacher of a culturally subversive wisdom according to which the unexamined life is not worth living. Like the Buddha, Jesus was an enlightened one who taught a subversive and alternative wisdom, the way that in his time, like our own time, was, and is, the road less traveled."[39] Robert Frost would be proud. Interestingly, the title of Frost's famous poem is actually "The Road *Not* Taken," which is exactly what I think the *actual* response has been to Jesus' way, despite what self-proclaimed Christians self-righteously believe.

Wisdom asks, "How shall I live?" Primarily through his parables and aphorisms, Jesus answered that question in a way that largely transcends his original audience. Borg argues that "the most certain thing we know about Jesus is that he was a speaker of great one-liners and a teller of stories."[40] (Je-

38. Ibid.
39. Borg, ed., *Jesus at 2000*, 11.
40. Borg, *Jesus in Contemporary Scholarship*, 147.

sus was apparently the inspiration for Henny Youngman, a fellow Jew, who is noted for his great one-liner, "Take my wife . . . please." This could explain why we have lost evidence of Jesus' marriage to Mary Magdalene; someone took her.) His teachings are the "guts" of his life, which are unfortunately omitted from the later creeds. It was a new way of "seeing," "centering," and "living." It was also a new way of being in relationship to God, one that is not dependent upon convention or institutions. For some, his wisdom was "good news," for others . . . not so good. In short, Jesus' wisdom taught a way of "transformation."[41] Let's be frank, shall we: Jesus' wisdom is *not* good news for gun dealers, anti-immigration zealots, and people who are rude to waiters. People who steal candy from babies, however, and thus are fighting against childhood obesity, are actually following Jesus' subversive wisdom. Kudos to them.

There was no Fox News in Jesus' day, however, I understand there was a conservative political-religious news channel called CML News (which is articulated as "Camel News" in honor of the vowel-free Hebrew language). For about three years it ran never-ending stories about "scandals" surrounding Jesus of Nazareth. They didn't like the fact that he was, as Borg also suggests, a social prophet. Jesus was critical of the economic, political, and religious elites of his day. Occasionally a church member of mine will tell me he or she doesn't think the church should be involved in politics. Really? Tell that to Jesus. He really pissed off some folks, which is what got him killed. He constantly challenged what theologian Walter Wink calls the "domination system" of his day. Taking away the theological baggage associated with the Christ of faith, the Jesus of history was very much in line with the great prophetic tradition of ancient Israel. They all had one thing in common: their opposition to oppression and exploitation of the poor and downtrodden.

The elites in ancient Israel primarily used the "purity system" to oppress the peasant class. Borg also calls this "the politics of holiness."[42] The gap between the rich and poor in that day was even more pronounced than the gap in our culture today:

> The governing class, the top one percent of the population, received about fifty percent of the wealth. The top ten percent (the governing class plus retainers and merchants) received about two-thirds. The remaining ninety percent (mostly peasants) produced

41. Borg and Wright, *Meaning of Jesus*, 69–70; Borg, *Jesus, a New Vision*, 97–116.
42. Borg, *Jesus, a New Vision*, 86.

most of the wealth, yet retained, due to taxation and land owner-
ship by the elites, only about one-third of their production.[43]

Today's peasants dis-enjoy about the same lack of wealth. (For a study of
America's peasant class, visit your local Wal-Mart Super Center.) Jesus'
prophetic rhetoric was generally aimed against "wealth, religious ideol-
ogy, the purity system, hierarchy and patriarchy, the temple and Jerusalem
itself—not as the center of Judaism, but as the center of the urban ruling
elites, who were also the temple and purity elites."[44] Borg calls Jesus and the
former prophets of Israel "God-intoxicated advocates of social justice."[45]
The label "God-intoxicated" is one of my favorite Borg-isms. This seems to
support one of my favorite theories that remains tucked away in my God-
intoxicated brain: that alcoholics and drug addicts are merely folks who are
looking for higher spiritual experiences.[46]

There are two issues surrounding the use of the word "prophet" that
need to be addressed briefly. The first relates to the common way many
contemporary Christians understand a prophet. They tend to see a prophet
as one who foretells the future, as if they have a crystal ball. In reality, a
prophet is someone who looks at events in history and makes predictions
based on those events. The notion that some of the Old Testament prophets
predicted Jesus' life is, to use a Bill Mayer term, "religulous."[47]

The second issue concerns what has been a very important topic
in historical Jesus studies: whether he was an *eschatological prophet* or a
non-eschatological prophet. "Eschatology" is the branch of theology that is
concerned with the "end times." An eschatological prophet, therefore, is
one who announces the end. The question is whether Jesus saw himself as
the prophet who was making this announcement *for his time.* Borg says no,
and he supports his answer with three reasons. First, Jesus historians are
skeptical that Jesus ever referred to himself as the "coming Son of Man."
Second, Jesus was very involved in the social and political crises of his time
and place. An eschatological prophet would have been more otherworldly
in his concerns. Third, as Borg writes, "belief in the imminent end of the
world among the followers of Jesus arose with belief in the second coming,

43. Borg, in Hoover, ed., *Profiles of Jesus*, 134.

44. Ibid, 135.

45. Borg and Wright, *Meaning of Jesus*, 71.

46. Smith, "Do Drugs Have Religious Import?"

47. This is a combination of the words "religious" and "ridiculous."

which clearly developed after Jesus' death."[48] There are other scholars who make other arguments, but I don't have a man crush on them. I'll just side with Borg for the time being. Resistance is futile.

Finally, Borg argues that Jesus was a movement founder. This doesn't mean he was trying to begin a brand new religion; it does mean he was passionate about a renewal or revitalization of the Judaism of his day. This is probably the reason Jesus seems to have been a little reluctant to share his message and ministry with non-Jews. In Mark 7:24–29 Jesus tells a Syro-Phoenician woman who is asking Jesus to perform an exorcism on her daughter, "The children have to be fed first. It isn't right to take the children's bread and toss it to the dogs." Her quick response rivals anything Jesus ever said: "Lord, even the dogs under the table eat the children's crumbs." He said, "Good answer!" and then tossed the demon out of her daughter's body. Biblical scholars suggests this story is authentic because it's a little embarrassing, and it also reveals the fact that Jesus was very much into his "social location." I also prefer to think it reveals Jesus' awareness that Syro-Phoenicians were mostly a bunch of a-holes.

Jesus' movement, of course, eventually became the Christian church, and yet if we had asked Jesus where he wanted "Christianity" to go, he would have answered, "Huh?" Still, his movement was not, as Borg says, "accidental"; it was "a deliberative embodiment of his alternative social vision, one that was inclusive and egalitarian."[49] The bottom line is that Jesus was a charismatic, healing, subversive, never-eats-alone badass. Who wouldn't want to be part of his movement?

Take a Picture . . . It Lasts Longer

So you and I hop in a time machine, set the dial for Palestine about 28–30 C.E. Of course, it would be dangerous for most of us to go there because our skin tone, hair style, and physical height would make us stick out like a Mormon missionary at Woodstock. We would also have very little way to communicate in their native tongue so we would have to keep our mouths shut. The food and water would make us puke. We would have to be willing to let go of our human waste in less than sanitary conditions. Air conditioning consists of a shade tree and nudity . . . which reminds me of a personal story. I remember being in Israel in the summer of 1988 when we

48. Borg, *Jesus in Contemporary Scholarship*, 27.
49. Borg, ed., *Jesus at 2000*, 11.

experienced a heat wave that produced temperatures over ninety degrees *in the middle of the night.* We had no air conditioning in our youth hostel, so we took our thin mattresses outside and stripped down to our boxers and briefs and prayed for a slight breeze as we tried to sleep in a pool of sweat. On second thought, I'm not hopping into a time machine!

If we were able to follow Jesus around with our smartphones and cameras, what would we record about the historical Jesus, the man, stripped of all his theological baggage? (First of all, we would hope that his friends are not heathen bikers who don't like their pictures taken.) How would we describe him? In this chapter I have included the views of just a few of the scholars who have had a great deal of influence on my spiritual-intellectual journey. You may have read others that have helped you to sketch a portrait of Jesus. As our most generous teachers like to say during class discussions, "There is no right or wrong answer." Perhaps, but that's no excuse for giving up the quest to discover who Jesus might have been and, more importantly, who he can be for us today.

In conclusion, I will offer one more quote from my man crush, Marcus Borg. In his book *Jesus: Uncovering the Life, Teachings, and Relevance of a Religious Revolutionary,* Borg relates a television interview in which he was given fifteen seconds to answer the question, "What was Jesus like?" He answered:

> Jesus was from a peasant class. Clearly, he was brilliant. His use of language was remarkable and poetic, filled with images and stories. He had a metaphoric mind. He was not an ascetic, but world-affirming, with a zest for life. There was a sociopolitical passion to him—like a Gandhi or a Martin Luther King, he challenged the domination system of his day. He was a religious ecstatic, a Jewish mystic, for whom God was an experiential reality. As such, Jesus was also a healer. And there seems to have been a spiritual presence around him, like that reported of St. Francis or the present Dalai Lama. And as a figure of history, Jesus was an ambiguous figure—you could experience him and conclude that he was insane, as his family did, or that he was simply eccentric or that he was a dangerous threat—or you could conclude that he was filled with the Spirit of God.[50]

Incidentally, on the cover of Borg's book *Jesus* is *Christ the Redeemer,* the statue of Jesus in Rio de Janeiro. Now that's a Big Jesus.

---

50. Borg, *Jesus,* 164.

A Meditative Interruption

The following is a condensed version of a sermon I preached on October 27, 2002, at First Christian Church (Disciples of Christ), Big Spring, Texas, after I returned from visiting the Jesus Seminar in Santa Rosa, California.

THE JESUS SEMINAR IS sponsored by the Westar Institute, a religiously oriented think tank that began in 1985 under the direction of Robert Funk, a former Disciples of Christ minister. Funk has fashioned the Seminar into a reputable organization. There are several things about the Seminar that make it unique in its approach to the study of religion.

First, it consists of a relatively large group of scholars who seek *consensus* with one another. This is truly remarkable because, historically, most scholars have done independent, although peer-reviewed, research, sitting in their ivory towers, writing books and articles to be read only by other scholars. Second, they make every effort to *communicate* their work to the general populace. You can go to their website, attend their meetings, and read their books, and you will be able to keep up with their work. Third, they work *democratically*. They actually vote on their findings. Finally, their goal is to be as *objective* as possible. That is, one's opinions, biases, and even faith perspectives are not allowed to stand without sufficient rational evidence to support them.

As you can imagine, an objective, unbiased approach to the Bible by a large group of scholars has an interesting effect on the results of their research. It has the effect of *minimizing* the amount of information upon which they can find consensus. They end up with the "greatest common denominator." In math, this is the highest number that can be divided into a set of two or more numbers. The Jesus Seminar's quest is to find the amount of information that a large group of scholars can agree upon, which can be very minimal.

For about fifteen years, the Seminar focused solely on the historical Jesus' reported words in the Gospels. They attempted to come to a consensus about what Jesus may or may not have said. Their results may startle or even upset you. They concluded that we can only be confident that about eighteen percent of the sayings attributed to Jesus in the Gospels were actually spoken by him. This doesn't mean Jesus couldn't have said more, but again, a consensus can only lead to the greatest common denominator.

Eighteen percent may not sound like much. In my opinion, however, the words of Jesus included in that eighteen percent are extremely powerful and provocative. They are enough to recultivate our faith if we choose to follow them. Most of us could spend the rest of our lives trying to live up to that eighteen percent. So I choose to respond to the findings of the Seminar this way: They have done us a favor in that they have simplified our religion. They have narrowed down the teachings of Jesus to a level that we ought to be able to grasp.

One of the Fellows said something at the Seminar that struck a chord with me. He said, "Less is more." Could it be that the "less" the Seminar has given us is actually "more" than we could ever hope to achieve? From my perspective, those who read the Bible as if every single word applies to us today have more or less spent their faith journeys mired in confusion, overwhelmed by it all. Our religion has been presented to us in such a complex and heavy way that it has weighed us down and neutralized us. Karen Armstrong, the author of the book *The History of God*, once told an audience that as a Catholic nun she became *weary* with God and religion. Isn't that what happens when we make religion so vast and complicated that only the scholars can understand it?

"Less is more." This phrase was originally spoken in 1959 by Ludwig Mies van der Rohe, a German-born American architect. He was a "minimalist." An architectural minimalist designs buildings that are simple and understated. These buildings take less time to design and build and they utilize space better. Maybe we need a religion that is simple and understated so that we don't get bogged down in too many details, requirements, creeds, etc. Maybe we could utilize our time better with a minimalist religion, although there would still be *plenty* to do.[1] If we just start focusing on the bare minimum of what Jesus taught, we are still faced with a lifetime of contemplation, meditation, struggle, study, and, hopefully, growth.[2]

1. See Jesus' conversation with a lawyer in Matthew 22:34–40. Here Jesus suggests that "all the Law and the Prophets depend on . . . two commands": love God and love your neighbor.

2. See Funk et al., *Five Gospels*.

5

Emergence Christianity
and the Reference Point

*Jesus needs to be saved from Christians who have slimmed him down
or fattened him up or otherwise converted him into our own image.*[1]

Swimming with Dolphins

MY OLDEST DAUGHTER, CHRISTEN, is upset because I have yet to mention
her in this book. Christen is a beautiful, petite young lady with a sweet,
gentle spirit. This is code for "passive aggressive." I asked her to tell me
about the most interesting thing she has done lately, and she said, "I went
swimming with dolphins." Apparently people do that sort of thing. I would
be afraid of rabies. I asked her what was so great about swimming with
dolphins and she just looked at me in disgust and asked, "Have you ever
been swimming with dolphins, Dad?" I said, "No, I'm afraid of dolphin
rabies." She said, "I don't think dolphins get rabies." I responded, "Maybe
not, but dogs do, and how do I know a rabid dog won't jump into the swimming pool while I'm swimming with dolphins?" "Dad," she said with exas-
peration, "you don't swim with dolphins in a swimming pool." My response
was stated with impeccable logic: "No, I don't, because I'm afraid of rabid
dolphins."

1. McLaren, *Generous Orthodoxy*, 110. Many readers might conclude that I have
slimmed down Jesus a little too much in this book. In reality he's lost a lot of weight on
his own climbing Zeppelin's stairway to heaven. Or was that Jacob's ladder?

I have had a few once-in-a-lifetime experiences of my own, such as digging in Israel, attending an REM concert, fishing for goldfish in a Chinese restaurant lobby, and seeing Bob Dylan in concert . . . after he turned seventy years old. Apparently singers at an advanced age are indecipherable . . . Nah, I'm not going to state the obvious. However, I've never been swimming with dolphins. All kidding aside, the next leg in my spiritual-intellectual journey has been almost as exciting to me. Like swimming with dolphins, I have felt a little out of my element on this leg of my journey. I almost said I feel like a fish out of water, but a dolphin isn't really a fish and I didn't want to confuse the reader. I'm talking about my recent flirtation with "Emergence Christianity"[2] (EC), which its followers claim is more of a "conversation" than a movement.

EC is a *postmodern* phenomenon dominated by Generation X folks and younger. As a Baby Boomer, I am always trying to reboot my philosophical outlook to postmodernism because my default outlook is deeply rooted in modernism. What is postmodernism? The *Stanford Encyclopedia of Philosophy* says postmodernism is "indefinable." "However," it also says "it can be described as a set of critical, strategic and rhetorical practices employing concepts such as difference, repetition, the trace, the simulacrum, and hyperreality to destabilize other concepts such as presence, identity, historical progress, epistemic certainty, and the univocity of meaning."[3] Yep, it's indefinable. So I'm still learning. Nevertheless, the question I have in this chapter is, "How, if at all, is EC helping us to understand Jesus for our time and place?" Before I offer a response to that question, let me first *attempt* to offer an explanation of Emergence Christianity.

In January 2013 my wife and I traveled to Memphis, Tennessee, for a national gathering of self-described EC leaders, participants, and curiosity seekers. The keynote speaker was Phyllis Tickle, the former religion editor at *Publisher's Weekly*, who is now, even in her advanced years, a spokesperson for EC. Phyllis' lectures at this conference were based almost word for word on her book *Emergence Christianity.* She spoke for hours without any notes and delighted the crowd with her charm, sharp wit, and lucid mind. Some of the major players in EC were there, including the hosts of the event, Tony

2. There are variations on the word "emergence" used in this book. This is because the words "emergence," "emergent," and "emerging" are used interchangeably at times, but other times there are distinctions among the users of the various labels. For a discussion of these labels and the general history and description of the movement, see "Emerging church."

3. Aylesworth, "Postmodernism."

Jones and Doug Pagitt. I also spotted Brian McLaren, Nadia Bolz-Weber, Lauren Winner, Bruce Reyes-Chow, and Jay Bakker, to name a few. Jay, of course, is the son of Jim and Tammy Faye Bakker. My wife and I met him as he walked out of the elevator we were about to enter. I'm pretty sure he still remembers us. My wife met Nadia, who told her to get a tattoo on one of her breasts, which is way beyond my expectations of what should occur at a religious conference. From my perspective, I also saw today's version of the ecumenical movement at this gathering. The ecumenical movement of the twentieth century sought to unify Protestant denominations, with the larger aim of unifying all of the world's Christians. Most people assume that the prospects of a successful ecumenical movement are summed up in the immortal words of George H. W. Bush: "Not gonna happen."

I love ecumenism. In fact, I joined the United Church of Christ in 1990 at least partially because they are much more ecumenical than my former spiritual home, the Southern Baptists. Today's Southern Baptists are *anything but* ecumenical. They are about as ecumenical as a pit bull in a chicken coop. What I saw at the EC national gathering in Memphis, however, puts the United Church of Christ and the ecumenical movement of the twentieth century *to shame*. At this gathering I met people who were UCC, Episcopalian, Baptist (of the moderate variety), Presbyterian, Cumberland Presbyterian, United Methodist, Disciples of Christ, Evangelical Lutheran, Catholic, Pentecostal, charismatic nondenominational, noncharismatic nondenominational, and folks from abroad. The only groups I did not personally encounter were Orthodox Christians, those from the Church of Christ (non-instrumental), and Tom Cruise. The point is that I met folks from all across the theological and denominational spectrum. I'm pretty sure most of them were there to add more friends to their Facebook page. I know I was. Seriously, there is obviously something interesting, if not exciting, occurring in Christianity today in many parts of the world. Emergence Christianity, however one defines it, is happening in places like New Zealand, Europe, Africa, and South America. It's also happening in Siberian labor camps, but documentation has been suppressed. It's sort of like swimming with dolphins . . . although I have no reference point for that.

The Peri-Normal

To understand Emergence Christianity, if in fact that's even possible, one must first understand the *peri*-Emergence. As a prefix, "peri-" means "about," "around," "enclosing" or "near." (A peri is also a beautiful fairylike being of Persian mythology, represented as descended from fallen angels and excluded from paradise until their penance is accomplished. Unlike the stories in the Bible that refer to fallen angels and paradise, this is obviously fabricated nonsense.) Tickle suggests that the peri-Emergence consists of those events in the last one hundred and fifty years or so that have led up to what she calls the "Great Emergence." She includes in her list the Azusa Street Revival (Pentecostal) and the Social Gospel movement, the Iona and Taize communities, churches in pubs and other counterintuitive places, Vatican II and liberation theology, Christian music festivals, and anything that smells like "alternative" worship. She describes the peris, or periods of buildup that precede major events in history, in terms of a pot being heated on a stove. Eventually the pot's contents go from hot to boiling.

Speaking of music festivals, one of the most visible manifestations of EC today is the Wild Goose Festival, which began in 2011. It is a four-day gathering "rooted in the Christian tradition" that focuses on justice, spirituality, music, and the arts. Many of the "big names" in Emergence and progressive Christianity are there. My wife and I have not made the trip yet because it looks like people sleep in tents and use porta-potties. The last time I used a porta-potty was for my bachelor party in 1980. My next doctor's checkup was not good. The wild goose, by the way, is the Celtic symbol or metaphor for the Holy Spirit. In the season of Easter 2013 my congregation in Louisville, Kentucky, held its own Wild Goose Festival. We began worship with the sound of a wild goose call and my sermons focused on the wild, dangerous, unpredictable nature of "chasing the wild goose" rather than the bland, safe, predictable act of "following the Holy Spirit." The biggest difference I can tell is that following the Holy Spirit leads to good works whereas chasing the wild goose requires the ability to fly in formation.[4]

Other than new and innovative faces of Christianity, the other thing that has occurred during the last 150 years is the destabilizing of Christian *authority*. This has happened particularly in terms of the authority of Scripture, brought to us by the Protestant Reformation and its assertion of *sola scriptura*; although a similar phenomenon has occurred in the Roman Catholic Church, where the authority of an infallible papacy has also diminished. In terms of Scripture, however, its authority began to erode in the face of challenges to its literal teachings about slavery, women, and

4. See Batterson, *Wild Goose Chase.*

LGBT concerns. The LGBT movement may prove to be the last nail in the coffin of an absolutist and literalist view of Scripture. Gay marriage will soon be a reality in all fifty states, which of course will destroy traditional marriage and convert all our children to homosexuality. It's like left-handed people corrupting righties; it's inevitable.

According to Tickle, this is not the first time in our religious history that major paradigm shifts have had their roots in "peri" events of previous generations. In Tickle's scheme, we see something "great" happening about every five hundred years. She quotes Anglican bishop Mark Dyer, who said that "about every five hundred years the church feels compelled to hold a giant rummage sale."[5] My current congregation holds a rummage sale every year because, well, we will all be dead in five hundred years. Tickle's scheme looks like this:

- The Great Transformation (first century C.E.)—Jesus and the beginning of Christianity

- The Great Decline (sixth century C.E.)—the decline of the Roman Empire[6]

- The Great Schism (eleventh century C.E.)—the schism between the Christian East and West

- The Great Reformation (sixteenth century C.E.)—the Protestant Reformation

- The Great Emergence (twenty-first century C.E.) Emergence Christianity[7]

Obviously, this scheme or pattern is somewhat arbitrary. Tickle has looked at the major events in our history that have occurred every five hundred years, yet one could just as easily do this every year or every thousand years. Also, these are events in *our* religious and cultural history and therefore could be described as myopic. Nevertheless, arbitrary or not, to use another less sanitized analogy, the church needs to take a crap at least every five hundred years, wipe its ass, flush the contents, and think about eating healthier.

---

5. Tickle, *Great Emergence*, 16.

6. She also links this period with Gregory the Great and the rise of monasticism. Tickle, *Great Emergence*, 21.

7. Tickle, *Emergence Christianity*, 17–21.

As I have reflected upon Tickle's understanding of the roots of Emergence Christianity, I have concluded that the peri events are those happenings and movements that push the proverbial envelope within Christianity. These are the events that move history forward and eventually become closer to the *norm*. Thus, the phrase "peri-normal" that began this section. (I didn't want you to miss that mastery of wordsmith-manship.) Movements and events that were once considered edgy and rejected by the mainstream are now at least partially accepted in the mainstream. As newer and edgier manifestations of religion push the envelope even further than before, groups that were once considered cutting edge become more like kindergarten scissors: they can still cut, only not as sharply as before.

What we have then in every era in Christianity, as well as every other major religion in the world, is a dance between the *core* and the *edge*. My favorite tattooed clergyperson, Nadia Bolz-Weber, defines emergence as "innovative edges." She writes:

> If we visualize the . . . Church . . . as consisting of both the core and the innovative edge, then we can see how needed a mixed economy of church can be for the vitality and survival of the tradition. The core holds the history, the tradition, and the money. It includes the ecclesial structures, the traditional churches that have existed for generations and are dying off, the newer and livelier suburban churches, the seminaries and colleges, and the para-church organizations. The midsection would be composed of youth, campus, and outdoor ministries—any ministry consisting mostly of younger people. The innovative edges then are emerging churches, multicultural ministries, and any ministry being established outside of the structure of the (denomination), especially by seminarians and laity in response to their context . . . The only way for the edges to survive is with the liturgical, theological, and financial resources of the core. The core, in turn, needs the life that is brought back to it from the edges in order to not atrophy.[8]

Personal disclosure: After hanging out with EC types for a few days in Memphis in 2013, my wife and I decided to get tats. I now have a beautiful representation of a blue jay, my Native American animal guide, perched upon my right shoulder. My life has totally changed.

So what do we find on the "innovative edges" of Christianity today? Sometimes we find gimmickry, for sure, but often we find *authenticity*, one of the buzzwords in the EC conversation. When it comes right down to

8. Bolz-Weber, "Innovating with Integrity," in Snider, ed., *Hyphenateds*, 5.

it, people who identify with EC are people who are looking for ways to be Christian in an authentic way in their time and place. As the Episcopalian priest Stephanie Spellers spells it out (sorry, I couldn't resist):

> Emerging churches are communities that practice the way of Jesus within postmodern cultures . . . I usually explain that emergence is not a style; rather, it is a paradigm shift whereby even the most basic elements of Christian practice, faith, tradition, and identity—worship, mission, community, scripture, formation—are translated through a postmodern lens and adapted to come alive in context.[9]

Emergence Christianity is difficult to define, yet, like other things that are hard to define such as beauty, love, and goodness, we know it when we see it. There are several characteristics that most Emergence Christians have in common.

First, they tend to be skeptical of institutional Christianity, even if they belong to a specific denomination. Denominationally affiliated Emergence Christians are often referred to as "hyphenateds." For example, I am an aspiring UCC-Emergent. We meet in a secret cave outside Cleveland, Ohio, where we share peanut butter crackers and Blue Moon on tap (our version of the Lord's Supper).

Second, they prefer as much of a non-hierarchical structure within their group as feasibly possible. Common wisdom suggests, however, that *someone* has to be in charge. In my congregation, for example, the babies are in charge, although I have no trouble stealing their candy when they get too power hungry.

Third, unlike goofy fundamentalists, they are comfortable with science. This is code for: "We are okay with our genetic relationship with other primates and all the other creatures on this planet and beyond." With the exception of llamas. We refuse to believe we are related to llamas.

Fourth, ECers have a penchant for paradox, such as "the last will be first, and the first will be last."[10] Some people argue that people who like paradoxes are just people who either can't make up their minds or who want it both ways. I say that people who like paradoxes are people who desire to confuse the masses even as they bring clarity to the confused.

---

9. Spellers, "Monocultural Church in a Hybrid Word," in Snider, ed., *Hyphenateds*, 18–19.

10. Matthew 20:16 (NRSV).

Fifth, the EC crowd shies away from oppositional terms such as "liberal" and "conservative." They wish everyone would hold hands and drink Coca-Cola and sing about harmony on an acre of groomed greenery. If it were me, I would only hold hands and sing with those who drink Diet Coke. But that's just me.

Sixth, they are very astute in their use of technology. They are obsessed, for example, with those little microphones that hug the side of their faces, which I often mistake for really big moles or warts.

Finally, they are liable to try *anything* in worship.[11] Shameless plug: My congregation also has a tendency to try new things in worship. Please join us this Sunday morning.

This gives us an idea about what Emergence Christianity looks like, but what does *Jesus* look like in this postmodern context? Wait for it . . . wait for it . . . Actually, I failed to mention that male Emergence Christians all wear horned-rimmed glasses, cool hats, and sport well-groomed goatees and ubiquitous tattoos. I have no idea what EC women (other than Nadia) look like because there aren't enough women in the movement to create a consistent look. Or people of color, but we won't go there right now.

Pastors Gone Wild

By the title of this section I am not implying that pastors frequently go partying on spring break and, after being plied with liquor, are easily coaxed into exposing their chests. I am implying, however, that sometimes pastors get together, have a few drinks, and talk smack about parishioners. We also talk about such things as Phyllis Tickle's books. If we take for granted the validity of the peri events that have led to what Tickle calls "The Great Emergence," then when did we first become conscious of the possibility that something new was stirring the pot, or at least the little bowls, of Christianity? Cultural movements are often inspired and fueled by youth and young adults; Emergence Christianity is no exception. Tony Jones, a leader in the EC conversation, relates the story of the "beginning" of EC in his book *The New Christians*. On June 21, 2001, Jones and a group of young pastors including Doug Pagitt, the head of the Young Leaders Network, convened for a conference call to discuss the future of their "movement." (Tickle says this happened in 2000. I think someone's book editor needs to do a better job.) They were looking for an identity. He writes, "We'd already

11. See Webber, *Ancient-Future Worship*.

been tagged with phrases 'emerging church' and 'emerging leaders' in years past, and those phrases came up again on this conference call. In the midst of the conversation, we settled on a variant of that word: we'd call ourselves 'emergent.'"[12] The name took root (pardon the future pun . . . wait for it . . .) when someone noted that the future of a forest depends not on the health and vitality of the treetops but on what is "happening down below on the ground where the emergent growth is."[13] Later, the group began a website, www.emergentvillage.com.

One of the most pivotal events in the early history of EC, however, occurred when Brian McLaren, who would become known as the father of Emergence Christianity (I'm still waiting for a mother), published a very provocative book titled *A Generous Orthodoxy*. In my opinion, this book set the tone for the ecumenical and theologically generous spirit of the EC conversation. There is seemingly no branch or perspective or theological corner that is off limits to the EC seeker. The subtitle of his book says it all: *Why I Am a Missional, Evangelical, Post/Protestant, Liberal/Conservative, Mystical/Poetic, Biblical, Charismatic/Contemplative, Fundamentalist/Calvinist, Anabaptist/Anglican, Methodist, Catholic, Green, Incarnational, Depressed-Yet-Hopeful, Emergent, Unfinished Christian.* I dare him to add "Mormon," "Jehovah's Witness," and "Scientologist" to an updated edition of his book . . . just to freak people out. The most important part of that subtitle is the word "unfinished." EC proponents are very reluctant to be pigeonholed as any particular *kind* of Christian; they just want to be a *new kind* of Christian.[14] They are very much in the seeker mode even if they understand themselves as intentionally Christian.

Mainline Protestant leaders, who have seen their own tribes dwindle in numbers over the past few decades, have taken notice of this nascent movement within the larger church. Perhaps the most famous story in regard to mainline awareness of EC concerns the former archbishop of Canterbury, Rowan Williams. Phyllis Tickle records this story in her book *Emergence Christianity*:

> The story—whether an ecclesial myth or otherwise—goes that the archbishop . . . was on an airplane when he read [*A Generous*] *Orthodoxy* and that he said, once he had finished reading, that all

12. Jones, *New Christians*, i.

13. Jones, *New Christians*, xviii; and Tickle, *Emergence Christianity*, 100.

14. McLaren, *New Kind of Christian*; idem, *New Kind of Christianity*; and Jones, *New Christians*.

he really wanted to do was buy up all the available copies of the book, hire a fleet of airplanes, and air-drop those copies all over the United Kingdom. Because, he is reported as having said, "This is what my people need to know, for God is indeed doing a new thing among us."[15]

I'm pretty sure the Anglican Church would be sued for head injuries more than the Roman Catholic Church has been sued for kiddie porn if they decided to do such a drastic thing.

Of course, not everyone is so enamored with McLaren, Tickle, Pagitt, Jones, and company. Mark Driscoll, the founding pastor of Mars Hill Church in Seattle, who was formerly identified with EC, said this in reference to the movement:

> There is a strong drift toward the hard theological left. Some emergent types [want] to recast Jesus as a limp-wrist hippie in a dress with a lot of product in His hair, who drank decaf and made pithy Zen statements about life while shopping for the perfect pair of shoes. In Revelation, Jesus is a prize fighter with a tattoo down his leg, a sword in His hand and the commitment to make someone bleed. That is a guy I can worship. I cannot worship the hippie, diaper, halo Christ because I cannot worship a guy I can beat up. I fear some are becoming more cultural than Christian, and without a *big Jesus* who has authority and hates sin as revealed in the Bible, we will have less and less Christians, and more and more confused, spiritually self-righteous blogger critics of Christianity.[16]

Driscoll is a new-Reformed new Calvinist, which just means he believes a lot of us are going straight to hell. Screw him. Brian McLaren says that if we reject Driscoll's depiction of a wimpy Jesus we may unintentionally protect and uphold a

> white supremacist, colonial, Eurocentric, Republican or Democrat, capitalist or communist, slave-owning, nuclear bomb-dropping America-first, organ-music stained-glass nostalgic-sentimental, anti-science know-nothing simpleton, prosperity-gospel get-rich-quick, institutional white-shirt-and-tie, Native American-slaying genocidal, cuddly omnipotent Christmas, male-chauvinist, homophobic 'God-hates-fags,' South African pro-apartheid, Joe-Six-Pack, anti-Semitic Nazi, anti-Muslim Crusader Jesus.[17]

15. Tickle, *Emergence Christianity*, 101.
16. "7 Big Questions."
17. McLaren, *New Kind of Christianity*, 123.

Now that's a Jesus I can worship! Not. Driscoll is obviously an unapologetic follower of Big Jesus. By the way—and this should not surprise us—Driscoll also believes women should be subservient to men. His wife just needs to kick his ass.

Driscoll is right about the drift toward the theological left, however. Most of those who are self-identified with EC were former inhabitants of theologically conservative evangelical (if not fundamentalist) congregations and denominations. Because of an evolving ecumenical spirit and a social conscience, they have found a greater affinity with theologically progressive groups. One of the most interesting things that happened at the gathering in Memphis my wife and I attended in January 2013, however, was some criticism from the left concerning some of Tickle's positive remarks about Pentecostal and charismatic expressions of Christianity. Personally speaking, giving kudos to conservative Christianity, even in a subtle way, gives me the willies and makes me feel icky. I had to take a shower afterwards. But that's just me.

One reason I have an affinity with Emergence Christianity, even if I have yet to receive my membership card, is that my religious journey sounds a lot like EC. I was emergent before Emergence was cool. As previously noted, I grew up as a conservative evangelical with Southern Baptist, nondenominational charismatic, and Assemblies of God pit stops along the way before I became a mainline liberal Protestant. I was never entirely comfortable in the conservative setting, however. The first sermon I ever preached was titled "Christian Unity," and I delivered it in an Assemblies of God church. Imagine that. My ecumenism was already trying to *emerge* in a church that values ecumenism about as much as I value rattlesnake rugs. Today, I may not be as theologically generous as McLaren and company, and yet I completely understand why someone would want to drift toward the theological left, especially if higher education is involved. Furthermore, I would love to meet someone who began their Christian career as a theological progressive, went to a liberal arts university or mainline seminary, and *then* became more conservative or fundamentalist. I would like to shake their hand and congratulate them for turning the world upside down.

To illustrate how critical many conservatives are of Emergence Christianity, listen to Scot McKnight, a friend of McLaren's, and who is generally supportive of EC (although critical at times), as he expresses an "urban myth" about EC folks in a tongue-in-cheek way:

It is said that emerging Christians confess their faith like mainliners—meaning they say things publicly they don't really believe. They drink like Southern Baptists—meaning, to adapt some words from Mark Twain, they are teetotalers when it is judicious. They talk like Catholics—meaning they cuss and use naughty words. They evangelize and theologize like the Reformed—meaning they rarely evangelize, yet theologize all the time. They worship like charismatics—meaning with their whole bodies, some parts tattooed. They vote like Episcopalians—meaning they eat, drink, and sleep on their left side. And, they deny the truth—meaning they've got a latte-soaked copy of Derrida in their smoke- and beer-stained backpacks.[18]

Sounds like some really cool people . . . but what do they think about Jesus?

A New Simplicity on the Far Side of Complexity

I hope my brief summary of EC will give the previously uninformed reader an incentive to look deeper into the movement. Personally, I often tell people that the writings produced by self-described Emergence Christians in recent years are among the *freshest* material I have ever read. An alternative way of looking at EC writings is, however, to understand it as rehashed or more palatable evangelicalism. To use the words of Dr. Roger Ray, pastor of Community Christian Church in Springfield, Missouri, the EC writers are just "polishing the turd" of evangelicalism. I guess this still implies a sense of "freshness." They may not be as fastidious about avoiding unnecessary bullshit as the historical Jesus scholars are. After all, they are more theologically oriented than Funk and company. And yet, compared to most other pastors and scholars who fall under the evangelical umbrella, well, let's just say that I need fewer showers after turning a few pages from their books. In

---

18. McKnight, "Five Streams of the Emerging Church," In this article, McKnight draws upon the work of Gibbs and Bolger in their book *Emerging Churches*, who define EC in this way: "Emerging churches are communities that practice the way of Jesus within postmodern cultures. This definition encompasses nine practices. Emerging churches (1) identify with the life of Jesus, (2) transform the secular realm, and (3) live highly communal lives. Because of these three activities, they (4) welcome the stranger, (5) serve with generosity, (6) participate as producers, (7) create as created beings, (8) lead as a body, and (9) take part in spiritual activities." Another great resource for understanding some of the general characteristics of EC proponents is Tony Jones' *The New Christians*. He offers twenty "dispatches from the emergent frontier" throughout his book.

particular, EC writers seem to want to take Jesus *beyond evangelicalism*, or as I like to call it, beyond Big Jesus.

For the remainder of this chapter I will briefly describe a sample of Emergence Christianity's portrayal of Jesus. As in the previous chapter, which highlighted some of the views of Jesus from a historical perspective, this is not meant to be a comprehensive summary. Nevertheless, it will read well with a cold brew in hand. I might as well begin with Brian McLaren, the old man of EC. I would start with the elder Phyllis Tickle, but in her books on EC she really doesn't touch on the Jesus question except to point out that Jesus made us change our clocks: "The birth, public ministry, teachings, crucifixion, and resurrection of Jesus of Nazareth as Messiah would cause even the epochs of human time to be re-dated, and this by believers and nonbelievers."[19] Now, you know a dude is a real badass if he causes epochs to be redated!

In *A Generous Orthodoxy*, McLaren lists and describes "the seven Jesuses" he has known. First, there is the Conservative Protestant Jesus, who saves us by dying on the cross. This is likely the first Jesus most of us met as children. Revealing a total lack of imagination, I call this the "Sunday School Jesus." It makes me wonder if perhaps we should bar children from church. Think about it: If we aren't allowed to drive until the age of sixteen, vote or join the military until eighteen, and drink until twenty-one—because this protects us from making bad choices—then maybe we shouldn't be allowed to contemplate joining a religious organization until we are old enough *not to be brainwashed*.

The second Jesus McLaren met as a young adult is the Pentecostal/Charismatic Jesus, an "up close, present, and dramatically involved in daily life" Jesus. I met this Jesus as a young adult as well. I can actually speak in tongues. So can you. Repeat after me: "Shunkatamata, shuntalmalaka," etc. Now go lay hands on someone and they will automatically be "slain in the Spirit." (Note: Do not practice this on the elderly.)

Through Catholic writers, McLaren then met the Roman Catholic Jesus, whose suffering and dying on the cross "changes forever the whole equation of existence." I married an ex-nun, so I can say pretty much the same thing.

Fourth, McLaren discovered the Eastern Orthodox Jesus through the writings of Dostoyevsky and Tolstoy. This Jesus "saves simply by being

19. Tickle, *Great Emergence*, 26.

born." They make up for their simplified view of Jesus with colorfully decorated sanctuaries.

Fifth, as a young man, McLaren was introduced to the Liberal Protestant Jesus, where the focus is on the words and deeds of Jesus (that which takes place between his birth and death), and naptime is synonymous with worship.

McLaren then recounts his introduction to the Anabaptist Jesus, whose followers also "find the heart of the gospel in the teachings of Jesus," focusing primarily on Jesus' nonviolence and peacemaking ministry. Anabaptists don't make good soldiers.

Finally, McLaren met the Jesus of the Oppressed, the Jesus found in liberation theology, particularly in his readings and travels to Latin America.[20]

After summarizing the many Jesus' he has met in his life, McLaren offers the following observation:

> In short, I tell the story of my encounters with Jesus to say that now, after many years of following Jesus and learning from many different communities of his followers, I'm just beginning to arrive at a view of Jesus that approaches the simple, integrated richness I knew of him as a little boy—picture Bible on my father's lap, flannel graph characters on my mother's easel, and a pure, child-like love welling up within me. You could say I'm finding *a new simplicity on the far side of complexity*. I am a Christian because I believe the real Jesus is all that these sketches reveal and more.[21]

As I read this I was reminded of Marcus Borg's characterization of a person's journey from the childhood stage of precritical naivety through the critical thinking stage of adolescence and adulthood to, finally, the postcritical naivety stage, when one can hear the stories of the Bible as "true stories" even while knowing that they are not literally true.[22]

Finally, McLaren asks, "Why not celebrate them all?" In *A Generous Orthodoxy* he does just that. He produces "a richer, multidimensional vision of Jesus," acknowledging that "Christians of each tradition bring their distinctive and wonderful gifts to the table."[23] In my opinion, this book set

---

20. McLaren writes about the "Rebel" Jesus—a first cousin to the Liberation Theology Jesus—in *Everything Must Change*, 227–36.

21. Ibid., 73–74. Italics artificially inserted by yours truly.

22. Borg, *Meeting Jesus Again for the First Time*, 17.

23. McLaren, *Generous Orthodoxy*, 74.

the tone for thinking about Jesus in Emergence Christianity and has also had a ripple effect in other corners of the Christian landscape, particularly in more progressive expressions of the church that are more open and inclusive of diverse viewpoints.

In his book *A New Kind of Christianity*, however, McLaren extracts a small but important sliver of generosity in order to position his understanding of Jesus more firmly in the progressive tribe. Sounding less naïve and more critical (and yet always generous and kind toward those who disagree with him), McLaren claims that "just saying the name 'Jesus' doesn't mean much until we make clear which Jesus we are talking about." "Jesus can be a victim of identity theft," he says.[24] (Wouldn't you love to see the actor Jason Bateman, star of the movie *Identity Theft*, cast as Jesus in a movie? Chew on that for a few minutes.) We are tempted "to remake Jesus into just about anything we like." He quotes Annie Lamott, who said that "we like a Jesus who hates the people we hate and likes whatever we like."[25] (The only people I dislike are slack-jawed fools, door-to-door encyclopedia salespersons, and motel attendants who like to short-sheet future inhabitants of room 137. Don't ask.) McLaren's task, it seems, is to set Jesus in a more appropriate *and biblical* context so that we won't use his name "in vain." May I just point out the possibility that Christians who misuse Jesus to judge and condemn others are breaking the commandment in the Old Testament about "taking the Lord's name in vain." Thus, they are without a doubt going to hell.

At the beginning of *A New Kind of Christianity*, McLaren lays out the "overarching story line of the Bible" as presented in traditional Catholic and Protestant theology. We began, he says, in a state of absolute perfection in the Garden of Eden, but then we "fell" into original sin. I prefer to call it a "fall upwards," because I like paradox. Seriously, if "sin" entered the world when the human race developed a moral conscience, then that is a good thing. I think we should celebrate "the fall" like we celebrate Christmas and Easter. Perhaps we could do so in autumn. Just sayin'. After the fall, no matter how or when it occurred, the human race has been in a state of condemnation. We need a savior; therefore Jesus came to earth, died on the cross, and rose from the dead. Salvation is now offered to us. Those who accept the offer find heaven; those who reject it find hell or damnation.

24. McLaren, *New Kind of Christianity*, 119.
25. Ibid., 121.

McLaren argues that this is a story line produced by a "Greco-Roman paradigm." He describes this paradigm as that which was initially shaped by Plato's cave analogy. We "descend" into the cave of illusion and "ascend" into philosophical enlightenment. It's sort of like saying, "We have to hit rock-bottom before we can go up." This is why people who were really "bad" make really "good" Christians. It's why, if this all holds true, I'm due a lot of accolades when I stand in front of God's judgment seat! McLaren also suggests that the Greco-Roman paradigm results from a "constitutional" interpretation of the Bible. This is probably the way Supreme Court Justice Antonin Scalia interprets the Bible—as a "strict constitutionalist." Right. McLaren then asks, "Can we dare to wonder, given an ending that has more evil and suffering than the beginning, if it would have been better for this story never to have begun?"[26]

McLaren, who has clearly moved to the theological left (as many in Emergence Christianity have), argues that we need to remove Jesus from this erroneous overarching story line and place him elsewhere. He calls Jesus "a living alternative to the confining Greco-Roman narrative in which our world and our religions live, move, and have their being too much of the time."[27] We need to instead place Jesus within a three-dimensional biblical narrative: "the Genesis story of creation and reconciliation, the Exodus story of liberation and formation, and the Isaiah story of new creation and the peace-making kingdom."[28] This Jesus, he says, is far more "wonderful, attractive, compelling, inspiring, and unbelievably believable than Jesus *shrunk and trimmed to fit within*" the Greco-Roman understanding of perfection, the fall and condemnation, and the offer of salvation that leads either to heaven or hell.[29] This is the Jesus described in McLaren's book *Everything Must Change*, where the violent, apocalyptic Jesus of the second coming is replaced with a Jesus noted for his "peace, love, truth, faithfulness, and courageous endurance of suffering."[30] Earlier, McLaren begs his readers not to "make what [he's] saying ridiculous by calling it a 'flower child' theology."[31] Let's not. Mark Driscoll doesn't like the hippie Jesus and he might get mad.

26. Ibid., 34–35.
27. Ibid., 126.
28. Ibid., 128.
29. Ibid., 136.
30. McLaren, *Everything Must Change*, 146.
31. Ibid., 142.

In *Why Did Jesus, Moses, the Buddha, and Mohammed Cross the Road?*, McLaren engages in interfaith dialogue, tackling the tough question of Christology. He notes that high Christology "has produced in practice far too many Christians with an elevated sense of superiority." The possible danger of high Christology is that it can lead to a sense that one's religion, theology, and God are superior to others, which doesn't exactly engender constructive dialogue with people of other faiths.[32] Rather than proposing a "weaker" Christology, however, McLaren calls for a "deeper, more vigorous, more robust Christology" that redefines "strength" (power) "in light of Christ's strength-through-weakness, gaining-through-losing, rising-through-descending."[33] This sounds really good, but I hope it's not just polishing the turd . . .

But Can He Turn a Staff into a Snake?

If Brian McLaren is known as the father of Emergence Christianity, what do his "children" say about Jesus? Doug Pagitt, the head pastor at Solomon's Porch in Minneapolis, Minnesota, and my favorite avid runner, confesses to "rethinking Jesus" in his book *A Christianity Worth Believing*. People who run have a lot of time to think because running, like other mindless activities, requires very little thinking, which is a redundant thing to say. (This is why my best sermon ideas come to me while walking on the treadmill or sitting on the toilet—although the latter exercise, for me, often requires my full attention.) Over the years Pagitt has evolved in his understanding of God, humanity, and sin, basically rejecting the traditional evangelical understanding of original sin (i.e., McLaren's Greco-Roman paradigm), which produces a chasm between us and God. He admits, however, that this left him in a quandary about what to do with Jesus:

> The Greek version of the Christian story provides an ideal place for Jesus: He is the one who connects us with God. He is the bridge. He is our way out of our depraved state. He is the blood sacrifice paid out for our redemption to appease the blood God. But if there is no cosmic court case, why do we need Jesus? If there is no gap, why do we need Jesus? If sin is really our "dis-integration" with the

32. McLaren, *Why Did Jesus, Moses, the Buddha*, 135.
33. Ibid., 137–38.

life of God and not an ontological problem of our humanity, why do we need Jesus?[34]

To answer his own question, Pagitt rejects the Greek view of God in favor of a Hebrew understanding that depicts an "integrated" God who brings healing and wholeness to all of creation. Fortunately, he finds Jesus "right at the center of it," claiming that "the whole Bible *is* the Jesus story."[35] The story of Jesus in the New Testament, he claims, is a replay of Jewish history:

> Jesus is born in a totally impossible situation to a young mother, reminiscent of Abraham and Sarah giving birth to Isaac in their old age. Jesus survives a childhood slaughter and is sent off to Egypt, just like Moses. Jesus faces temptation in the wilderness, just like the nation of Israel. Jesus goes to a mountaintop and speaks for God, just like Moses. Jesus is the good shepherd, like David. Jesus takes on the priests like the prophets did. Jesus heals and raises the dead in the way of Elisha and Elijah. The story of Jesus is a Jewish story in all its fullness.[36]

Even Jesus' name would impress a first-century student of Jewish history. The Hebrew version of Jesus is "Jeshua" or Joshua. In the Old Testament, Joshua was the one who completed the work of Moses. Moses may have been called to lead the Israelites out of Egyptian bondage, but it was Joshua who led them into the "Promised Land." Pagitt doesn't use this term, although many people do. We need to be careful using it in the midst of the contemporary conflict between Israelis and Palestinians, who both lay claim to this little piece of real estate. (My solution is to kick them all out and give the land to the Romani people. Any further attempts at humor at this point would be completely inappropriate.)

Jesus' audience, therefore, would have heard *just in his name* the fulfillment of God's promises. (Admittedly, when people hear my name they hear something totally different. I remember the first time my name became significant. It was in the CB radio era of the 1970s. There were many nights that I heard my name mentioned through multiple frequencies followed by the general pronouncement, "Let's go kick his ass." CB radio saved me.) Whether or not Jesus *actually* represents a fulfillment of God's promises—if in fact there is a God who makes such promises in the first place—it is nice

34. Pagitt, *Christianity Worth Believing*, 174–75.
35. Ibid., 176.
36. Ibid.

to have a historical framework in which to interpret the Gospels' presentation of Jesus. The only promise I want to hear coming from God is that reality television will soon go the way of the dodo bird. If I wanted reality I would go outside and meet my neighbors. Nevertheless, thanks, Doug. Now, keep running and thinking and leading congregations who sit on couches rather than pews. By the way, read Pagitt's "Inventive Age" series because nothing spells "inventive" like Christian couch potatoes . . . (Just kidding, Doug.)

Duck Dynasty

One of my favorite duck hunters is Tony Jones, theologian-in-residence at Pagitt's Solomon's Porch. I recently purchased a white Lab (i.e., "silver bullet" Lab) named "Jake" because Jones said Labrador Retrievers are the best dogs in the world. (Jake would be a great dog if he didn't shed, eat as much food as he does, and chew on my O'Neill flip-flops.) As a duck hunter, Jones knows a thing or two about the blood and guts—the messiness—of life, and he applies this willingness to get his hands dirty to his work as a blogger, author, and teacher. He is even willing to admit how messy his personal life has been by talking openly about going through a divorce. Theologically, like McLaren and Pagitt, he has "blown a hole" in the Augustinian doctrine of original sin, creating opportunities to reinterpret the role of Jesus particularly in terms of the doctrine of the atonement.[37]

Jones has been one of the primary interpreters of Emergence Christianity. In his book *The New Christians* he offers twenty "dispatches from the Emergent frontier" (the subtitle of his book), many of which reveal a postmodern "messiness" as he rejects the sterility of modern Christianity. The first three "dispatches" will suffice to illustrate how willing he is to shoot something and have his dog go fetch:

- Emergents find little importance in the discrete differences between the various flavors of Christianity. Instead, they practice a generous orthodoxy that appreciates the contributions of all Christian movements.

- Emergents reject the politics and theologies of left versus right. Seeing both sides as a remnant of modernity, they look forward to a more complex reality.

37. Jones, *Better Atonement*.

- The gospel is like lava: no matter how much crust has formed over it, it will always find a weak point and burst through. (I'm pretty sure Tony was popping a zit at the time he wrote this. Or maybe not.)[38]

Jones is slightly more theologically conservative than I am—for example, he continues to believe in a literal, bodily resurrection of Jesus, polishing the turd on occasion—as are most of the Emergence folks, and yet I get the feeling that if he could travel back through time and produce a reality television series about Jesus, *he would censor nothing*:

> If we affirm that "Jesus is truth," then truth had lice, toe jam, smelly armpits, and a daily bowel movement [and, I would add, zits]. It is unquestionably more difficult to think of truth in these terms. Too often, when we consider truth, it's as an ethereal concept that hovers somewhere above the earthly realm, untouched by the *messiness* of human existence. But the beauty of the Christian faith is that truth is just the opposite: it's incarnate (made flesh) in an actual human being—a human being who happened to live before the era of advanced personal hygiene. Is it disrespectful, even blasphemous, to consider Jesus' bodily habits? No. To the contrary, it's bad theology and possibly even unchristian to avoid the realities of God's incarnation in Jesus of Nazareth. Ours is not a spit-shined God who, as a "human," walked a couple inches off the ground so that his feet never got dirty. No, he had smelly feet and, I imagine, even stubbed his toe on occasion.[39]

I'm pretty sure the duck call–producing Robertsons of West Monroe, Louisiana, would be proud.

I Wanna Be a Reference Point

In terms of their Christology, Emergence Christian writers are all over place. Their interests are far ranging and varied, colorful and creative, inspiring and provocative. In terms of the question "What does Emergence Christianity think about Jesus?" they seem to employ a "scattershot" approach—which is not a bad approach. I haven't owned a gun since my

38. Jones, *New Christians*, 8, 20, 36

39. Ibid., 161. I used italics on the word "messiness" because it is the universal symbol of *pay attention to this freaking word*. Jones is absolutely obsessed with messiness. In his Introduction to *An Emergent Manifesto of Hope*, Jones describes Emergent Village as "A mess. A beautiful, *good* mess."

youth, but I remember my daddy telling me, "Son, all you need for protection is a shotgun. Just point it in the general direction of the bad guy and he will haul ass away from you. If you have to shoot, a shotgun won't miss." (My dad should be appointed as Gun Czar of America.) Despite their scattershot approach, there are some common themes in EC Christology.

First of all, there is a lot of interest in reinterpreting or reevaluating the traditional doctrine of the atonement. I have already pointed out that McLaren, Pagitt, and Jones are all grappling with this issue, clearly dissatisfied with the way orthodox Christianity continues to present it to the masses as if it were "gospel." In my opinion, atonement theory is *the* turd of orthodox Christianity. Rather than polish it, we need to flush it because it belongs in the sewer lines of historical Christian theology. Again, there are differences in the EC approach to this issue. Dan Kimball, to give one example, agrees with the doctrine of substitutionary atonement, and yet asserts that focusing exclusively on the atonement distracts us from being "kingdom-minded" disciples.[40] Karen Ward admits that there is no "emerging theology of the atonement." Rather than rely on words to define the atonement, she says we should explore the use of "art, ritual, community, etc." Also, because none of us understand "God's true nature," we should talk about the atonement "with a grain of salt, knowing that if we get saved in virtue of our correct theology, we're all in trouble."[41]

At the Emergence Christianity 2013 conference in Memphis, Tennessee, Phyllis Tickle noted that atonement theory is the one big issue Emergence Christians need to address in the present moment. It is clearly *the* theological issue of the day, much as homosexuality is the great social issue of the day. By the way, I'm done trying to appeal to people's "better angels" in terms of their approach to homosexuality and gay marriage. To those heterosexuals who claim that homosexuality is a choice, my question is, "When did you *choose* to be heterosexual?" Personally, I remember that day clearly. I was in the first grade and I met a little redheaded girl named Judy. I was so enamored with her that I convinced my folks to name our new German shepherd puppy after her. The romance was never consummated, yet I knew beyond any doubt that I was a budding hetero.

If we feel compelled to scrap the doctrine of the atonement altogether, or at least in its traditional forms, then what do we do with Jesus? What role

40. Kimball, in Webber, ed., *Listening to the Beliefs of Emerging Churches*, 100–101.
41. Ward, in Webber, ed., *Listening to the Beliefs of Emerging Churches*, 163–64.

does he play in Christianity? Or, to ask it in another way, what would Jesus put on his own Wikipedia page?

Over the years I have dreamed about either starting a business or inventing something weird. On days when I'm sitting in my Adirondack chair on my front porch contemplating my future, inevitably my attention gets stuck on one particular thought as if my mind is a broken record. I imagine starting a bumper sticker company that produces the most original, imaginative, odd, and perplexing bumper stickers in the English language. Nothing much comes to mind except the following words: "I wanna be a reference point." Let this serve as my copyright to this slogan. If I see it on another car in the future I will tattle-tell on you. A reference point, of course, is an indicator that orients us in a general way. To some extent, anyone who has a Wikipedia page *is* a reference point for something. I don't have a Wikipedia page. But I want one.

If Jesus of Nazareth had a Wikipedia page *that he wrote*, what would he say? To what would he be referring? The answer, according to many writers in Emergence Christianity (and beyond), is *the kingdom of God*. I realize the phrase "kingdom of God" is not politically correct, yet, as the historical Jesus scholars have pointed out, Jesus' use of the phrase would have irked and threatened both Caesar and Herod. The phrase is as much political as it is religious. We could also refer to the "empire," "realm," or "reign" of God. Although I get the motive for using "kin-dom" of God, as some do, I draw the line there because it just looks like someone hit the wrong key on their keyboard or they are missing the letter "g."

To claim that Jesus considered himself to be a reference point for the kingdom of God is important because many Christians assume Jesus of Nazareth had a habit of referring to himself, particularly in terms of divinity or as the Messiah. The general scholarly consensus is that Jesus was not so self-focused. His words and deeds are not pointing to the kingdom of *Jesus*. He is not a reference point that points to his own self. He is, instead, a reference point that points to the kingdom of *God*. As the Zen Buddhist saying goes: "Don't confuse the finger pointing to the moon with the moon itself." Jesus is the finger that is pointing to something beyond himself (something "near" or "within" all of us, if we believe the ancient Gospels).

EC writers are not the only group of thinkers that use Jesus as a reference point for God's kingdom, but they do so frequently and eloquently. Eddie Gibbs and Ryan Bolger, in their book *Emerging Churches*, point to the work of N. T. Wright as one of the contemporary scholars who have answered the question "What is the gospel?" for Emergence Christians. He claims that it is Jesus' announcement that the kingdom of God was arriving. I'm not a fan of N. T. Wright but I do recognize his creativity. He just seems to me to be better than most at polishing the turd.[42] Wright draws on Mark 1:15–16 to suggest that "at the outset of the Gospel narrative, the good news was not that Jesus was to die on the cross to forgive sins but that God had returned and all were invited to participate with him in this new way of life, in this redemption of the world."[43]

Emergence Christianity often distinguishes between the "personal salvation" message of traditional evangelicalism and the "kingdom" message of Jesus. One way they do this is by focusing more on the Gospels than the Epistles, the latter (as I noted previously) tending to be the primary source for evangelical sermons. EC writers are more interested in the question of how to follow Jesus rather than the question of what he has done for us in terms of salvation. The key word for many EC writers is "authenticity." "How can we be authentically Christian?" they ask. The answer has more to do with *following* Jesus than *believing in* Jesus, a point that liberal-progressive Christians have been saying for a long time.

Furthermore, one of the common assertions in EC is that the traditional model we find in contemporary Christianity—believe, behave, belong (in that order)—should be replaced with the following order: belong, behave, believe. The emphasis in EC is on *belonging* rather than *believing*. The primary message is that God's kingdom is *big enough* for all of us, which contrasts with the orthodox message that one needs to *believe in Jesus' bigness* in order to be included in the kingdom of God. EC is therefore a "big tent" approach to Christianity and to Jesus' role in the religion. John Burke suggests Jesus' big tent approach is for the "global village"—only if, however, we refrain from judging others, invite people to "come as they are," and are not afraid to show God's grace in a "messy" world.[44] Jesus is not an exclusionary figure, as Big Jesus inevitably becomes, but a figure that serves as a reference point for something much bigger than himself: the kingdom

---

42. Gibbs and Bolger, *Emerging Churches*, 53. For more turd polishing, see Anderson, *Emergent Theology for Emerging Churches*, 96–116; Chalke and Mann, *Lost Message of Jesus*, 21–40; and McLaren and Campolo, *Adventures in Missing the Point*, 47–57.

43. Gibbs and Bolger, *Emerging Churches*, 54.

44. Burke, in Webber, ed., *Listening to the Beliefs of Emerging Churches*, 64–69.

of God. As Gibbs and Bolger conclude, "When a crisis of confidence hit the church, emerging churches retrieved the life of Jesus as a reference point."[45]

"Jesus is my Reference Point." Put that sticker on your bumper.

I submit that if people have "Christian" bumper stickers on their vehicles then they should do their best to be followers of Jesus. Quit pussyfooting around. Of course, trying to follow Jesus in our day is not easy because we don't always know how the way he lived in his setting translates into our setting. This is a big part of the postmodern Christian dilemma. However, one thing I am certain about is that "If people slap you on your right cheek, you must turn the left cheek to them as well" is as true for us today as it was for Jesus and his contemporaries, because nothing spells "Christian" quite like masochistic behavior. And that, my friends, is Emergence Christianity. Sort of.

---

45. Gibbs and Bolger, *Emerging Churches*, 64.

6

Jesus' Top Ten

Jesus did many other things as well. If all of them were recorded, I
imagine the world itself wouldn't have enough room for the scrolls
that would be written. (John 21:25)

"There are also many other things which Jesus did." And since He
did them, clearly they were not aimless, but had a divinely ordained
purpose. It might be asked why they are not recorded if such question-
ing were not anticipated in the selfsame verse. The answer is, that a
complete account, as one has said, would be practically infinite. "The
world itself could not contain the books that should be written." Nor
is this oriental hyperbole. The figurativeness of the language is obvi-
ous; but, as in all appropriate imagery, the symbolical setting serves
to press home the truth symbolized not only more forcibly than plain
matter-of-fact language, but as something transcending the literal
force of the image itself. In this case the theme is infinite, and is there-
fore susceptible of infinite treatment.[1]

Shifting Sand

THE ABOVE QUOTES SYMBOLIZE the hyperbole that surrounds Big Jesus.
Even after the writer of John's Gospel ran out of stories to tell (or fabricate),

1. Say what? Beacon, "Unwritten Things which Jesus Did."

he or she couldn't resist telling the reader that a man who only lived to about thirty years of age did so much in his brief existence that the paper trail about his life would put even the George W. Bush Library in Dallas, Texas, to shame. There is no way Jesus of Nazareth did more in his brief ministry than President Bush did in his eight years in the White House. After all, Bush had Air Force One and Dick Cheney; Jesus just had a borrowed donkey and Peter. (I apologize for all the penis references.) The purpose of this book has been to cut through some of the hyperbole that has accumulated over the last two thousand years in order to get a more sober perspective of the young Jewish peasant that admittedly left a mighty big footprint on the sands of human history. The problem with footprints in the sand, however, is that there is a lot of *shifting*.

I recently accompanied my family to the beach at Siesta Key in Florida. Believe it or not, this was my first trip to the state that resembles a penis. I simply never had reason to go there in the past. Still, it was interesting to be there during the week George Zimmerman was found "not guilty." I felt like I was in the "Twilight Zone." On what planet is it okay for someone to take the law into one's own hands, harass a young man who is walking down the street, and shoot him dead during a scuffle? In what universe does this equate to "standing your ground"? Why didn't that absurd law apply to Travon Martin more than it did to Zimmerman? Earth to Zimmerman: "From now on, stay in your pickup, dumbass."

Back to the beach . . . I had been to beaches before, mostly at the Texas Gulf Coast. I have done almost everything there is to do at a beach . . . except swim with dolphins. I'm afraid the dolphins might have rabies. On our visit to Florida I had a new beach experience: posing for professional family pictures while standing in the sand. I don't know if you have ever tried to be perfectly still while standing in the place where the sand meets the tide, but one is literally sinking. The sand shifts beneath your feet and because I had one foot closer to the Gulf of Mexico than the other, in no time at all I looked like a man with legs of uneven length because my right foot was sinking faster than my left foot.

Similarly, in this postmodern world the ground beneath our collective feet is constantly shifting. For example, there is inconsistency in the way our laws are written and applied. Just ask young African-American men like Trayvon Martin. Furthermore, our understanding of science and the development of technology is growing faster than the lobe in our brains that informs our sense of right and wrong. Our moral compass can't keep up with our technology. Philosophically speaking, we live in a rudderless age, which means (to switch metaphors) there is no longer a "firm foundation" for faith. Sing with me now: "How firm a foundation, ye saints of the Lord, Is laid for your faith in His excellent word! What more can He say than to you He hath said—To you who for refuge to Jesus have fled?" In our postmodern world, that is no longer a hymn we can sing with a straight face.

It is in this age that desperate Christians will do anything they can to give the impression that there is something solid and concrete about Christianity. With nothing really solid to build upon, however, it is in this age that Christianity becomes little more than a "name cult," an era when anything done "in the name of Jesus" carries with it an unquestionable authority. Christianity is almost forced to invent a false sense of absolute truth and authority because in reality these things no longer exist. They have long since sunk in the sand. Nevertheless, we hold on to Christianity's truth and authority as a baby holds on to a security blanket (or in this case a beach towel). It is in this age, therefore, that we promote Jesus to "lifeguard," hovering above us on the pedestal we have created for him, coming down from above to rescue us from drowning in our sins.

It is in this age, likewise, that we interpret Jesus' table fellowship with sinners in a way that puts him at the *head of the table* and gives him the power to forgive those who grovel at his feet, when in reality Jesus sat at table with fellow sinners in a non-hierarchical manner. It is in this age that the parable of the prodigal son is considered a story about *others* rather than the one who told the story in the first place. Jesus *was* a prodigal son, although our interpretive lens of Jesus is foggy from all the heavy breathing as we lust for the hyperbolic Big Jesus. We yearn for Jesus to come down from his lifeguard stand so we can invite him into our metaphorical hearts so that we can attain forgiveness for a misdiagnosed condition of sinfulness in order to punch our tickets for a land as fanciful and as shallow as Disney World. It is in such a misguided and misled age that the entire corpus of Jesus' mission is relegated to a splintery and bloody cross so that a deity with the virtue of a lurking vampire can drink the only source of blood that can bring atonement to one particular species on one specific planet in one tiny corner of an expanding universe. This is what happens when we attempt to build a solid foundation where one doesn't exist. Matthew's Jesus says, "But everybody who hears these words of mine and doesn't put them into practice will be like a fool who built a house on sand. The rain fell, the floods came, and the wind blew and beat against that house. It fell and was completely destroyed."[2] Whoever wrote this was instinctively aware of the fickle nature of religiosity. I can almost hear him whispering to Christians today, "Yes, I know none of this makes a lot of sense, but if we can just keep it going, if we can go against all the odds and all the evidence, if we can just keep preaching the same message, then maybe it will eventually harden and become indestructible against the waves of secularism, science, and sanity."

It won't harden, however. Instead the sand will keep shifting until the whole thing is washed out to sea. It was easier and even unavoidable in the ancient world to solidify one's beliefs because the ancients favored a world-view that consisted of three solid, unshifting tiers: heaven above, the flat earth at our feet, and the world below. The ancients lived in a metaphorical three-story building: God owned the building, Jesus managed it, the Holy Spirit maintained it, and the devil caused a lot of plumbing problems. This world no longer exists, nor did it ever. Our modern understanding of the cosmos has evolved to the point that the foundation for most of our religious beliefs and spiritual intuitions, rooted in the ancient worldview, are about as firm as the sand that continues to shift under our feet as we hold still for just *one more* picture . . .

Brittle Leaves

To switch metaphors again, the high Christology that threatens to drown Christianity in irrelevancy today is as susceptible to annihilation as the brittle leaves that have fallen from the holly tree that stands, ironically . . . firmly . . . in my front yard. Florida's "stand your ground" laws should apply only to trees. My holly leaves may be brittle and destructible, but when I step on them with my bare feet they hurt like hell. Likewise, Big Jesus, the one we created perhaps out of necessity, will not go away without first drawing blood. I use the word "necessity" because I believe that if we Christians didn't invent him, someone else would have. Although we put up a good front about how *solid* our faith is in Christ, the cruel truth is that even our faith or trust in an all-loving, all-good, and all-powerful God—our faith in a secure and life-giving universe—is vulnerable to nature's fickle fury and history's unpredictable events. For faith to crumble like a dry leaf, all it takes is a hurricane or a homicide or anything else that destroys our copasetic world.

2. Matthew 7:26–27 (CEB).

Humanity—the first and perhaps only self-conscious creature on this planet—is in a constant struggle to ignore the signs of insecurity all around us. We are aware of our possible demise as a species, as nations, as communities, as families, and, of course, as individuals. Unlike other creatures we are aware of our impending death. We see death as *the ultimate problem* rather than what it really is: *an ultimate solution* to the *actual problem* of having millions of creatures living on a spatially limited planet trying to do one thing above all else: reproduce. I did my fair share of reproducing; now, as they say, it's time to hang up my spurs. Death, often accompanied with suffering, makes room for life. It may not be the best system in the universe, but it's the one we have. And, according to the German mathematician and philosopher Gottfried Leibniz, this is "the best of all possible worlds." Suck on that Jupiter!

The various religions in the world approach the perceived problem of death in different ways. Almost all of them postulate an ultimate escape from death, including Christianity's heaven, Judaism's Olam Haba, Islam's Jannat, Wiccan's Summerland, and Hinduism's reincarnation. Personally, I'm hoping for reincarnation. I would love another chance to master Sudoku. Of course, they also propose various ways to "get there." For some, you just have to show up—"universalism" is the belief that all of us will enjoy the same fortuitous fate. In other schemes, however, a person has to either "do" something (or a lot of things) or "believe" something (or a lot of things) *or else*. I'm referring to hell, of course. Conservative Christians claim this is *my* final destination. In preparation for this journey I have made a beautiful hand basket.

I may live in a very unusual place and have very unusual experiences and know particularly unusual people, yet from my perspective the most prevalent view in our culture is that in order to attain heaven, or a favorable afterlife, one must "accept Jesus as their personal Lord and savior." I actually did this once. I prayed to Jesus,

> Look, I know you're busier than Santa Claus on a Christmas Eve. I know there are a lot of people who also want you as *their* personal savior. But by golly I don't want to roast in the fiery pit of earth's core for eternity because that would hurt. I know I've screwed up a few times and probably deserve eternal punishment. I mean, I once took my school's only bus on a joy ride on a Friday night. But my principal gave me three licks for that the next week. Isn't that enough punishment? Anyway, if you could find time in your busy schedule to put my name in that little book of yours, I would be

most appreciative. In fact, I will go to church and sing songs about you and give money so that they can run the air conditioner in the summer. I will also vote Republican so the godless homosexuals can't get married. Whatever it takes, I'm yours.

This is traditionally called "the Sinner's Prayer" and I believe I was saved within twenty-four hours after I said this prayer. (It takes a while for Jesus to process the paperwork.)

Opinions differ about what happens to those who do *not* accept Jesus as their personal Lord and savior, but that's a question that need not bother folks who are busy watching reality television. (I know I shouldn't criticize reality television so much because, after all, it is inexpensive to produce and it gives us a candid view of the lives of people who don't mean anything at all to me—except Snooki of course.) Having a first-century Galilean peasant as the guy who both compels part of humanity to change their calendar system and alters the personnel roster in the afterlife may not be the best system in the universe; still, it's the one we have . . . or it's the one most people in my neighborhood have. By the way, the planet Jupiter has a different system for "salvation" altogether. Jupiter's god, Jupiter, is still pissed off that he was usurped by Christianity's god during his tenure with the Roman Empire on planet Earth. A power hungry god, Jupiter now decides the fate of all Jupiterians, spending most of his evenings eliminating unbelievers with smartbomb-like thunderbolts. He rarely misses his target, however, in the event of a missed target he has to drink shots and chasers.

Jesus has become the religious version of American banks: he is "too big to fail." In economic theory, "too big to fail" asserts that certain financial institutions are so large and so interconnected that their failure would be disastrous to the economy, and so they must therefore be supported by the government when disaster looms.[3] I guess size *does* matter after all! Jesus—Big Jesus—has become so big, so ubiquitous, so ingrained in the theological psyche of what is now the Christian mainstream, that even I would fear his sudden demise or downsizing. If a document were to be unearthed that *proved* Jesus' true identity is more in tune with a Christology on the low end of the scale, I'm afraid mass suicide would ensue. Therefore, I propose that those of us in the progressive Christian tribe try to enlighten the masses *slowwwwwwwwwwwwly*.

3. "Too big to fail."

It's Okay If You Can Make a Song about It

The first thing I feel I must do is deconstruct C. S. Lewis' famous "trilemma." Lewis, who remains popular among evangelicals and mainline Protestants, tried to prove the divinity of Jesus by arguing that there are only three ways to respond to Jesus' self-proclamation that he is the Messiah, Lord, or even God: Jesus is either 1) a lunatic, 2) a liar, or 3) the Lord. This is also called the "mad, bad, or God" formula. This formula sounds nice and neat to people who believe human and dinosaur footprints are found in the same rock or that "freedom of religion doesn't mean freedom *from* religion," but it isn't as tidy a little argument as it seems. (The latter is a reference to Texas Governor Rick Perry, who apparently doesn't believe in the freedom to be an unbeliever. In his defense, I don't think he meant that he would execute secularists. At least I don't think he would.)[4]

Concerning the trilemma, my first objection is to note that Lewis takes for granted that Jesus *did* claim to be the Lord and/or divine. I don't have the time or the inclination to point out how ignorant this is of contemporary critical biblical scholarship. I'll just give the punch line in a way that would make a street punk proud: "Oh no he didn't!" (Pronounced *o no he di-int*.) To substantiate my claim, I will quote Paul Alan Laughlin from his book *Remedial Christianity*:

> He [Jesus] seems to have been much less explicit and definite about his own identity and role than later generations of Christians have been. Indeed, Jesus was very tight-lipped, vague, and even evasive about himself—except, of course, in John's late and embellished gospel. One reason for Jesus' equivocation is that he did not make himself the center of attention, as St. Paul and the Church later would, but constantly directed attention instead to God, God's fatherhood, God's will, God's actions, and above all God's domain.[5]

Jesus also tried to draw attention to God's new haircut on the day of his baptism, but everyone was afraid to look.

Second, Jesus may have been a little mentally ill because, let's face it, most of us struggle with our mental health from time to time—just as we do with our physical health. Due to the religious climate of first-century Palestine, if Jesus had a few "messianic complex" moments I think we can give him a free pass. Third, I'm not willing to argue that Jesus was an outright

---

4. "Gov. Rick Perry: 'Freedom of Religion Doesn't Mean Freedom from Religion.'"

5. Laughlin and Jackson, *Remedial Christianity*, 93.

liar (because I don't want to risk eternal punishment if it turns out that hell is a viable option), but I do believe it is possible to believe something about one's self erroneously.

Finally, just to freak out Lewis' devoted readers, Jesus may have been "the Lord" without even realizing it. I have actually toyed with this notion for myself. I mean, could it be that the Lord of the universe is about as unaware of that fact as a mentally challenged person is unaware of their mental handicap? To push this further: Is God even aware that he/she/it is God? "What if God was one of us, just a slob like one of us?" asks rocker Joan Osbourne. Yeah, what if God is one of our teenaged sons? Do you think he would know it while he's busy rummaging through his stash box? Play with that idea for a while.

To me, other than trying to figure out why pajama-wearing Major League baseball players need to use performance-enhancing drugs, the question of Jesus' identity is downright interesting. Years ago I heard the Christian rock pioneer Larry Norman perform in my hometown. I don't remember the songs he performed at that concert, but I have since been mysteriously drawn to his song "Outlaw." In this beautiful song, Norman offers five possible explanations of Jesus' identity: he was an outlaw, a poet, a politician, a sorcerer, or the Son of God. Norman, of course, affirms the fifth possibility with these words: "And that's who I believe he is, cause that's what I believe." Herein is the problem with allowing singer-songwriters to define something as important as Jesus' identity. They engage in circular reasoning! Circular reasoning (also known as paradoxical thinking or circular logic) is a logical fallacy in which "the reasoner begins with what he or she is trying to end up with."[6] Does anyone ever ask why we allow theologically untrained musicians to set the theological tone? At least Larry Norman, unlike C. S. Lewis, set his logical fallacy to music . . .

A Jesus for Every Christian

Okay, let's get down to brass tacks. Who was that Jesus fellow anyway? I'm pretty sure this book will never be placed on an Arlington barrister bookcase alongside first editions of Albert Schweitzer's *The Quest of the Historical Jesus*, Marcus Borg's *Meeting Jesus Again for the First Time*, or John Shelby Spong's *Jesus for the Non-Religious*. I have tried my best, however, to give a sense of my journey with Jesus from my evangelical upbringing through

6. "Circular reasoning."

my educational experience, focusing on the Jesus portrayed through the lenses of process theology, historical Jesus studies, and most recently Emergence Christianity. The search continues. As I have written on the chalk wall in my kitchen: "To search is to find; to find is to abandon the search." This is written directly above what a friend chalked about me—"Jimmy has a grandma"—because somehow it struck her as funny that a grandfather (which I am) would also have a living grandparent (which I do). The truth is, as I often tell folks, "In my family we breed early and often."

Why is the search for Jesus' identity important? It is important because the Jesus we perceive in our minds is the one we will strive to follow at least to some degree. The Jesus we imagine has a lot to do with how we treat other people, especially those who differ from us religiously, politically, economically, racially, and ethnically, and in terms of gender and sexual orientation. The Jesus we imagine has a lot to do with how we vote and our support or lack of support for war, gun control, human rights, the environment, immigration, and almost every other major issue that continues to polarize our nation and world. Carter Heyward speaks to the relevance and importance of Christianity's view of Jesus when she states:

> In a very real sense, there are as many images of Jesus, and as many feelings and thoughts about, as there are Christians. Just as one church or person can raise up an image of a Jesus Christ who requires that all homosexuals repent of their sexuality and be born again in order to be saved, so too can another church or person celebrate a Jesus Christ who was himself a lover of men like John the Evangelist and who is calling us to 'act up' on behalf of queer justice. This tension bears witness to both the power of the multiplicity of Jesus traditions to generate and regenerate images of Jesus and the power of the human imagination to construct whatever we think we need in order to make sense of our lives and world.[7]

Obviously, Heyward is suggesting that John the "beloved disciple" was gay. Not that there's anything wrong with that. By the way, I encountered an "Act Up" group in San Francisco one day in the mid-1990s. Not only did they lie down in a busy intersection and block traffic in front of a gay-hating church, they also took down the church's American flag and raised a rainbow flag in its place. Boys from West Texas don't see that kind of thing every day.

---

7. Heyward, *Saving Jesus From Those Who Are Right*, 16.

Who we understand Jesus to have been, for Christians, is not a subject we can leave to the experts hoping that some of their learned views will rub off on us because we live in a Christian culture. This is a subject that requires our full attention from the scholar in the ivory tower to the Sunday school teacher in the preschool class. This is not an easy endeavor. As Harvey Cox notes, "There has probably never been a period in which so many scholars—stimulated by new manuscript finds, the refinement of archaeological procedures, and new analytic methods—have been so preoccupied with the debate about who Jesus really was and have churned out so many options."[8] Nevertheless, we should at least give Jesus as much thought as my dog, Jake, gives to his next meal. Okay, maybe that's getting a little carried away, but you know what I mean.

As we think about this Jesus dude, however, it is not enough just to say what he isn't, or to spend most of our energy engaging in a postmodern deconstruction of the man from Nazareth. If we are going to catch the attention of our neighbors and those who are eavesdropping on our conversations from the booth behind us in the local Mexican food restaurant, then we need to have something positive to say. One way to do this is not to emphasize how Jesus is *less* than something, as Jesus scholars often feel obliged to do out of necessity and integrity. Instead, we need to emphasize how Jesus is *more* than something. I feel that might be more palatable to the sisters and brothers who sit in the pews of First Baptist Church of Anywhere on Sunday mornings. For example, to say that Jesus is "less than divine" sounds very negative and critical; to claim that he is "*more* than divine" (because "divinity" is a vacuous concept anyway) sounds less destructive. I realize I may have already lost some of my reading audience with my occasional profanity and subtly progressive views, but for those of you who have laid off the spicy tacos in order to avoid indigestion, let me share with you ten things about Jesus that I think make him much more exciting and less shifty and brittle than Big Jesus. I will present these sequentially in terms of the English alphabet, or, to put it in simpler English, "alphabetically." Also, in case you're wondering, I will not be referring to Ricky Bobby's "Dear Lord Baby Jesus."

8. Cox, "Jesus and Generation X," in Borg, ed., *Jesus at 2000*, 94.

Jesus' Top Ten List

More Than an American

About a decade ago, a couple of thick books were published one right after the other, leading me to think that the two authors had made some kind of wager to see who could best articulate the notion—using my words—that Big Jesus is as American as baseball, apple pie, and Wal-Mart. (I apologize to all hot dog aficionados. I'm guessing the French and Swedes think of Wal-Mart more than hot dogs when they think of "the land of the free and home of the brave.") The first of these books was Stephen Prothero's *American Jesus: How the Son of God Became a National Icon* (2003). The table of contents reveals the breadth of his discussion about Jesus. He portrays Jesus as enlightened sage, sweet savior, manly redeemer, superstar, Mormon elder brother, black Moses, rabbi, and oriental Christ. Because the book is already too big, he admits to omitting the Native American, Hispanic, gay, Christian Scientist Jesus or even the Jesus who had sex with Mary Magdalene (which would have been particularly titillating). The following year, Richard Fox published *Jesus in America: A History (Personal Savior, Cultural Hero, National Obsession)*. Fox offers a more historical approach, tracing the role and relevance of Jesus in America since the sixteenth century. One doesn't even have to read these books—although I did—to understand how Jesus is closely identified with American culture . . . by Americans of course. In reality, Jesus is no more our prized possession than the moon is, even if we *were* the first ones to arrive on the moon's surface. (Of course, we know this is a hoax. The first earthlings to land on the moon were the Mexicans, who established the Space Center in Houston long before Sam Houston helped procure Texas independence from Mexico. I think I read that right. Not really sure.) And yet, there seems to be a sense, at least to this red-blooded American, that Jesus is almost one of us, that American and Christian values stem from the same source.

Debates abound about whether we are a specifically Christian nation or a religiously pluralistic nation. The answer to that question (which I give as I hold my nose) is that we are a little of both. While noting that Christianity is obviously the dominant religious expression in America, Prothero suggests that pluralists see this as a problem, whereas the "Christian nation" crowd sees this as a positive development. Prothero writes:

> Each of these approaches misses much. The Christian nation camp
> overlooks the vitality of non-Christian religions in the United

States, while the multi-religious camp turns a blind eye to the public power exercised by the Christian majority. Both sides fail to see how extensively insiders and outsiders are improvising on one another—how Buddhists, Hindus, and Muslims are adopting Christian norms and organizational forms, and how Methodists, Baptists, and Presbyterians are taking up, however stealthily, the beliefs and practices of Asian religions.[9]

The truth is we are one of the most religiously diverse nations in the world, while at the same time one of the most Christian—at least in terms of labels. However, as my friend and colleague Reverend John Manzo of New Albany, Indiana, suggests, we should only use the word "Christian" as a noun, not as an adjective. Therefore, to call a nation "Christian" is a misuse of the word. I agree. The only time we should use the word "Christian" as an adjective is in relation to plumbing services that have a fish symbol on their window. After all, nothing spells "Christian" quite like a group of men who unclog our toilets. (That is a spiritual metaphor that has been neglected far too long.) Seriously, as Prothero suggests, "Any story of religion in the United States that fails to take seriously both Christians and non-Christians is bound to obscure as much as it illuminates."[10]

My larger point, however, is that Jesus is/was no more American than the Russian president. If any of us who sing "The Star-Spangled Banner" or drive Ford pickups or kill squirrels for fun think that our lifestyles resemble in any way, shape, or form the "Way" Jesus taught his ragtag group of first-century fishermen and prostitutes, we probably need a psych evaluation. To illustrate just how distinctly un-American Jesus and his disciples were, consider that they did *not* shop at Bass Pro Shop. So let's stop with the "American Jesus" nonsense. If he came back today in some weird second coming scenario, he would not come to America. He might call President Obama on the phone (or whisper in his ear with a "still small voice"), but I think he would avoid a land where people deny evolution, climate change, and the death of Elvis. So let's move on, understanding that Jesus is much more than a mere American. Before we do, however, let's read the words to an actual song called "American Jesus" by the appropriately titled band Bad Religion:

> I don't need to be a global citizen, Because I'm blessed by nationality, I'm a member of a growing populace, We enforce our

9. Prothero, *American Jesus*, 5–6.
10. Ibid, 7.

popularity, There are things that seem to pull us under, And there are things that drag us down, But there's a power and a vital presence, That's lurking all around, We've got the American Jesus, See him on the interstate, We've got the American Jesus, He helped build the president's estate, I feel sorry for the earth's population, 'Cause so few live in the U.S.A., At least the foreigners can copy our morality, They can visit but they cannot stay, Only precious few can garner the prosperity, It makes us walk with renewed confidence, We've got a place to go when we die, And the architect resides right here, We've got the American Jesus, Bolstering national faith, We've got the American Jesus, Overwhelming millions every day, He's the farmer's barren fields (In God), The force the army wields (We trust), The expression on the faces of the starving millions (Because he's one of us), The power of the man (Breakdown), He's the fuel that drives the Klan (Cave in), He's the motive and conscience of the murderer (He can redeem your sin), He's the preacher on T.V. (Strong heart), The false sincerity (Clear mind), The form letter that's written by the big computers (And infinitely kind), The nuclear bombs (You lose), The kids with no moms (We win), And I'm fearful that he's inside me (He is our champion), Yeah, we've got the American Jesus, See him on the interstate (We've got the American Jesus), We've got the American Jesus, Exercising his authority, We've got the American Jesus, Bolstering national faith (We've got the American Jesus), We've got the American Jesus, Overwhelming millions every day (One nation under God).[11]

More Than a Celibate

One of the more salacious questions surrounding Jesus concerns his sexuality. Obviously, because the church has attached the biological need to reproduce (and have fun) to the worst genre of sins, there seems to have been a monumental push (pardon the pun) to keep Jesus free from the pleasures of female (and/or male) genitalia. To put this in simple terms, if Jesus had been involved in the carnal pleasures then he would not be pure enough to be our savior. This of course borders on absurdity even if one considers the possibility that a stripped down, ready-to-crucify Jesus may have startled the crowd with an inappropriately placed hickie or, worse, a visible sexually transmitted disease.

11. From their 1993 album *Recipe for Hate*.

Protecting Jesus from the immorality of sex is rooted in the view of many throughout history that sexual activity is a necessary evil that has only one purpose: to procreate. And to think that Jesus may have actually procreated is one of those rare notions that stir the slumbering masses from their mass hallucinations of Jesus' perfection. It is fascinating indeed that folks think Jesus could not have been perfect if he had had sex on one or more occasions. I mean, come on, Jesus was a red-blooded American . . . I mean Jewish male. For him to not have sex is like saying Jeff Gordon has never gone full throttle on the racetrack. Cynthia Bourgeault, an Episcopal priest, articulates well the problem we have with a sexual Jesus: "We assume that Jesus was a celibate ascetic and have built our most cherished images of him on the basis of that assumption. If he was secretly sexually active, then he is either a failure or a fraud; either way our house of cards come tumbling down."[12]

Fortunately for our sanity, there have been occasional interruptions to our stupidity, including the rock opera *Jesus Christ Superstar*, Nikos Kazantzakis' novel *The Last Temptation of Christ*, and Dan Brown's novel *The Da Vinci Code*, all of which at least hint at the possibility that Jesus may have frolicked with Mary Magdalene between healings and exorcisms. I was a student at Hardin-Simmons University in 1988 when *The Last Temptation of Christ* came to the big screen. Along with a couple of friends, I broke through a picket line consisting primarily of West Texas Baptists who thought that Jesus could never have been tempted to have sex with Mary Magdalene. I'm sorry, but have you *seen* Mary Magdalene? Tony Soprano would have said, "Bada Bing!" The point is that Jesus *may* have been a celibate, but it is not important that he was one. As Bourgeault concludes, "The church's insistence on Jesus' celibacy and its defensive hysteria around the suggestion that this may not in fact be so are merely further evidence that from the start Christianity has gotten the Jesus path slightly wrong. If we truly recognized him for what he was, his relationship with a human beloved would be a cause for joy, not consternation.[13]

Jesus may have had sex. Get over it. It's not the end of the world. And even if it is . . . *what a way to go.*

12. Bourgeault, *Wisdom Jesus*, 78.
13. Ibid., 80.

More Than the Church

Who could forget the Church Lady on *Saturday Night Live*, played by Dana Carvey? The Church Lady skit featured Carvey (a man) as a holier-than-thou female host of the talk show *Church Chat*. Each week she interviewed a different celebrity, either the person who was guest-hosting *SNL* that week or fellow cast members who played the role of a celebrity. The Church Lady was good at uncovering the sins of her guests (often by referring to their "naughty parts"), offering quips that have become popular American idioms, such as "Well, isn't that special!" She also finished each episode with a funky little dance that seemed to imitate a clucking chicken. Carvey claims that his memory of the church ladies in his boyhood congregation inspired him to come up with the Church Lady skit. Carvey's character could be construed as sexist, although it roughly reflects the reality of church life. From my experience, there are always more elderly women than elderly men in congregations. This suggests that the stereotypically uptight, sin-obsessed judgmental elderly church member, who exists to one degree or another in almost every congregation in America, will more often than not be a woman. The men usually die before they get so crotchety.

The Church Lady is a caricature of not only elderly women in conservative congregations throughout America; in the view of younger generations, she is a caricature of the church itself. The church, in the view of younger folks, is archaic in its obsession with sin. I noted earlier that the younger generations see the church as hyper-conservative and judgmental, particularly in terms of gender and sexuality issues. If this portrayal of elderly Christianity is true— and I think it is to some degree—then many people who sit in padded pews on Sunday mornings understand Jesus in much the same conservative and judgmental way. To most Christians, Jesus and the church are linked together in ways that are not easily untangled. They are like flipsides to the same coin.

Despite this, there are a large number of younger Americans who are attracted to Jesus even as they hold up their noses at the institutional church. Harvey Cox, who taught a class about Jesus at Harvard University for many years, required his mostly Generation X students to write an essay in response to the question Jesus posed to his disciples, "Who do people say that I am?"[14] After reading many of these essays over the years, Cox conclude, "Although they have their doubts about doctrines and rituals, ministers

14. Mark 8:27 (NRSV).

and theologians, they retain a continuing fascination for Jesus . . . Generation Xers see Jesus as beyond or before churches and different from the doctrines they have heard about him."[15] Cox contends that these younger folks are looking for a deinstitutionalized Jesus. They are "famously suspicious of all institutions," he writes, "including governmental, educational, and religious ones."[16] No wonder, then, that Emergence Christianity, with its skepticism of institutions, is fueled largely by Generation X constituents.

Cox noticed two other characteristics about the religiosity of Generation X. First of all, this is the first generation to be fully aware of religious pluralism. Thus, they are open to outside voices on subjects that were once considered only the purview of insiders, such as the doctrine of Christology. Some people obviously still have a difficult time with people outside of Christianity telling us what they think about Jesus. One of the most infamous examples is a 2013 Fox News interview of Reza Aslan, a Muslim and a religious scholar with a PhD in the sociology of religions from the University of California, and author of the book *Zealot: The Life and Times of Jesus of Nazareth*. Fox News host Shannon Bream continued to prod him about why a Muslim would write a historical book about Jesus. Her most glorious moment occurred when she compared this to a Democrat writing a book about Ronald Reagan, furthering the unfortunate Republican mythology of Reagan's divinity.[17]

Second, Generation X has no problem picking and choosing from all faith traditions. To a large degree, because of their anti-institutionalism, pluralism, and smorgasbord approach to religion, this is the generation that gave us the "I'm spiritual but not religious" mantra. However, not all Gen Xers are so enamored with the "I'm spiritual but not religious" approach to religion. Lillian Daniel, a United Church of Christ minister from Chicago and a Gen Xer herself, admits that these people are "boring." She writes,

> If we made a church for all these spiritual but not religious people,
> if we got them all together to talk about their beliefs and their incredibly unique personal religions, they might find out that most
> of America agrees with them. But they'll never find out. Why?
> Because getting them all together would be way too much like

---

15. Cox, "Jesus and Generation X," in Borg, ed., *Jesus at 2000*, 93.

16. Ibid.

17. See Kaczynski, "Is This the Most Embarrassing Interview Fox News Has Ever Done?"

church. And they are far too busy being original to discover that they are not.[18]

(You have to love Lillian's brand of crotchetiness.) This approach to religion in general and Christianity in particular will probably continue to become more and more popular as our neighborhoods continue to become more and more diverse and the church continues to present a portrait of Jesus that is uncomfortably close to its own values . . . with or without the church ladies. The only thing I have to say to the young people and the "spiritual but not religious" crowd out there—regardless of one's age—is that Jesus was (and perhaps is) far more than the church generally portrays him to be. Not to sound too radical, but if the church ever understood what Jesus was all about, I suspect the walls would collapse either from anger or excitement. I would sure like a front row seat to that show.

More than a Conservative

Why is it that when the media interviews a representative of Christianity most of the time the talking head is a conservative evangelical or fundamentalist?[19] By the way, I have a hard time distinguishing between a conservative evangelical and a fundamentalist. As far as I can tell, they drink the same Kool-Aid. There also seems to be an equally disproportionate number of closeted homosexuals in their ranks. Not that there's anything wrong with that. Nevertheless, I often get the impression that media reporters wouldn't know a liberal-progressive Christian leader if he or she bit them in the ass (and yes, we allow females to do more than submit to their abusive alcoholic husbands). The only reason I am able to give these media mental midgets a free pass is because conservative-fundamentalists are just freaking *loud*. I think their philosophy is, "He who shouts the loudest has the most truth." It is very difficult to hear moderate or progressive voices in the religious marketplace today because there are too many Jerry Falwells out there (God rest his soul . . . seriously, rest for a long, long time, Jerry). My problem with the conservative-fundamentalist tribe is not just that I disagree with slick-back hairstyles, emotional manipulation, and constant begging for money. My real problem with these wonderful but

18. Daniel, *When "Spiritual But Not Religious" Is Not Enough*, 11–12.

19. Burchfiel, "'Progressive' Christians Say Media Coverage Skewed to Religious Right."

misguided Christians is that, to quote Iris Dement from her song "Wasteland of the Free" as she berates American conservatism, "They don't look like Jesus to me." And that's really my big beef with them. I don't mind that they are conservative or fundamentalist. I believe in religious freedom, so pound your pulpits and flap your floppy Bibles all you want as you blame hurricanes and wars on our tolerance of fags and the murder of fetuses. Just don't tell me Jesus was *like you*.

A conservative is someone who is reluctant to accept change, especially if it happens quickly. Conservatives favor the status quo and traditional values and customs. Synonyms for the word "conservative" include traditional, conventional, conformist, unadventurous, old-fashioned, and old school. I see *nothing* in that definition that even comes close to my understanding of Jesus. I'll make an exception to the word "diehard," which I found in an online definition of "conservative." Jesus was certainly a diehard *on the cross*. Maybe I'm flapping the wrong floppy Bible around.

Liberals, on the other hand, are by definition open and broadminded, tolerant (if not accepting) of different views, values, and customs. Liberals favor change and reform, freethinking and moderation. From an evolutionary standpoint, relative to conservatives, liberal-progressives are one more notch above our knuckle-dragging ancestors. According to studies conducted at New York University, Berkeley, and UCLA, liberals have more evolved brains and are slightly more intelligent across the board.[20] In contrast, Fox News viewers are not quite up to snuff on the news.[21] For his time and place Jesus was highly evolved. To call him a "liberal" is perhaps a bit too anachronistic. Still, if we have to choose between calling him a liberal or a conservative, well, we are forced to acknowledge the title of Scotty McLennan's recent book, *Jesus Was a Liberal*. McLennan begins his book by defining liberals as those who believe in "progress, tolerance, individual freedom, and the essential goodness of humanity."[22] The NRA believes in these things as well . . . and yet I still wouldn't want to be in their crosshairs.

McLennan then offers the punch line "Jesus was a religious liberal" before he offers the following explanation, which he then expands throughout his book:

> He [Jesus] came with a fresh new progressive vision, proclaiming
> again and again, "You have heard that it was said to those of ancient

20. Gellene, "Study Finds Left-Wing Brain, Right-Wing Brain."
21. "Study Finds Fox News Viewers Least Informed of All Viewers."
22. McLennan, *Jesus Was a Liberal*, vii.

times . . . but I say to you . . ." Instead of an eye for an eye, he asked us to turn the other cheek. Instead of loving just our neighbors, we were called upon to love our enemies too. He spoke of a new testament, distinct from the old testament that came before. When the apostle Paul described Jesus' new testament, he explained that it was "not of letter but of spirit; for the letter kills, but the spirit gives life." Jesus was not a fundamentalist in the sense of being a biblical literalist. He would break one of the Ten Commandments when he thought it was the most humane thing to do, as when he worked, healing people, on the Sabbath. As he clearly said, "The Sabbath was made for humankind, and not humankind for the Sabbath."[23]

So, my dear brothers and sisters, the media may ignore the liberal-progressive voices within Christianity today, and yet by doing so they ignore Jesus himself. And there's *a lot* wrong with that.

More Than the Creeds

I've led several congregations in my life as a clergyperson, most of them from the "E" side of the United Church of Christ. This refers to the Evangelical Synod of North America, one of the four predecessor bodies that joined in 1957 to form the United Church of Christ. These congregations are deeply rooted in German heritage and their style of worship tends to be very traditional and liturgical. Because of that, one of the most frequent criticisms I have heard over the years is that I don't include the Apostles' Creed in Sunday morning worship often enough. Truth be told, I sincerely dislike the Apostles' Creed and every other creed for that matter. One of the reasons is my non-creedal Baptist upbringing. Before the Fun-damn-mentalists hijacked the Southern Baptists back in the 1980s, a good Baptist was one who would neither recite an ancient creed nor sign a statement of faith. Traditional Baptists were fiercely independent and believed in a notion called "soul competency." We didn't need a creed written centuries ago to tell us what to believe.

The other reason I dislike the creeds so much is because they effectively gut the story of Jesus. As Tom Harpur, Canadian Anglican priest and journalist, points out, the ancient creeds tell us nothing about the kingdom of God, the central theme of Jesus' teachings. The social ethic of the Gospels is missing from the creeds, including the Golden Rule and his admonitions

23. Ibid.

to love and forgive. Furthermore, the creeds emphasize theological points that Jesus himself never taught. This compelled Harpur to write, "There is no doubt left in my mind that this is one more powerful reason why the ancient creeds should be retired from active duty and be replaced by others more truly authentic, honest, and clear."[24] Harpur does just this, publishing a creed in 1986 that effectively "polishes the turd," yet is much more palatable than the Apostles' and Nicene Creeds. Other viable options for the church today include the United Church of Canada's "A New Creed" and the United Church of Christ's "Statement of Faith." Or, you can go with the succinctly written bumper sticker creed that says, "God said it. I believe it. That settles it." No, no it doesn't.

Another anti-creed witness (and there are many) comes from the pen of Geza Vermes, a respected biblical scholar of the twentieth century, who said about the Nicene Creed: "The historical Jesus, Jesus the Jew, would have found the first three and the final two lines of the Christian creed familiar, and though not theologically minded, would have no difficulty assenting to them, but he would no doubt have been mystified by the remaining . . . lines. They appear to have nothing to do with the religion preached and practiced by him."[25] According to Vermes, Jesus would have raised a thick Mediterranean eyebrow if he had heard references to himself as "Lord" and "Son of God," claims about his eternal nature, his being of the same "substance" as God and our source of salvation, his incarnation and virgin birth, his resurrection and ascension, his role in the final judgment, and the notion that he should be adored and glorified with God and the Holy Spirit. If he parachuted into one of our liturgical worship services today and heard the creed spoken in unison he would probably ask, "Who are you guys talking about?"

Jesus is more than the ancient creeds. The creeds give us a vision of Jesus that no longer excites postmodern seekers, even if their omission from worship causes consternation and constipation among more traditional congregations. Along with Tom Harpur, I say we retire the creeds from active duty. Let's minimize the bullshit and maximize the lost art of integrity.

24. Harpur, "New Creeds," in Schwartzentruber, ed., *Emerging Christian Way*, 62–64.
25. Vermes, *The Religion of Jesus the Jew*, 209–10.

More Than a Human Being

To say that Jesus was more than a human being may sound counter to what I have been communicating in the rest of this book. I am not saying that Jesus was *not* a living, breathing, red-blooded human being; I am saying that he was more than that. I'm also not saying that this means he was divine, because, as I noted earlier, I have no idea what that means. If it means that he existed in heaven before he was born to the Virgin Mary, then I would conclude that no, he was not divine, yet he was definitely something more than your average human being. I assume he was also smarter than your average bear, but then, who isn't?

To say that Jesus was more than a human being means that he was more than our own *limited understanding* of what it means to be human. This suggests that our first task is to interpret who Jesus was coupled with an awareness of our inevitable failure in this endeavor. There is a good reason for our inevitable shortcomings in the quest to know the human Jesus. The recently deceased scholar Walter Wink warns all of us would-be interpreters and followers of Jesus to be aware of the Heisenberg principle: "that the observer is always a part of the field being observed, and disturbs that field by the very act of observation."[26] By the way, this is not the same Heisenberg who produces blue crystal meth on my favorite television series, *Breaking Bad*, although I imagine there is some strange connection. Regardless, we can never formulate a truly objective view of Jesus "as he really was." For some reason, everyone's Jesus turns out to be a lot like the observer, or at least the observer's idealized vision of what it means to be a human being.

Nevertheless, Wink claims that historical criticism is a tool that helps us recover a close approximation of the historical Jesus. He writes, "We do not need 'a final truth of history,' but only approximate truth backed up by evidence."[27] And what we discover from our quest for the historical Jesus is, he suggests, "the archetype of what it means to be human."[28] The quest for the historical Jesus is the quest for the *human* Jesus. And the quest for the human Jesus, he says, "is the hunger for one's own emergent consciousness."[29] After all, unless there is an ethical dimension to our quest

---

26. Wink, "The Myth of the Human Jesus," in Hedrick, ed., *When Faith Meets Reason*, 99.

27. Ibid., 100.

28. Ibid., 101.

29. Ibid., 104.

for the identity of Jesus, then what use is it? If its purpose is not to better humanity, then why endure the search? Wink claims that the recovery of Jesus' humanity, in contrast to the orthodox focus on his divinity, is a "sacred task." He then concludes with a personal confession: "No doubt a part of me wants to whittle Jesus down to my size so that I can avoid painful, even costly change. But another part of me is exhilarated by the possibility of becoming more human."[30]

At the end of the day, is not the purpose of Christianity—and all religions for that matter—to give us the tools to become *more human*, that is, to become *better* at being human? We should remember this the next time we engage in meaningless debates about the supernatural aspects of the biblical Jesus. I don't know about you, but none of that makes me more human. It just makes me more frustrated. For example, I tried to walk across a creek the other day—on top of the water—without getting my shoes wet. I was told that I just needed enough faith. So I prayed the Lord's Prayer, a rosary, spoke in tongues, and sung the "Gloria Patri." The first step went okay, and then I looked down and noticed my shoes were untied. "Never look down," as they say.

More Than a Male

Let me set one thing straight: Jesus was a human being and he had a male member. That's right. Jesus was a dude. I have no idea what he did with his male member, whether he was sexual or asexual, whether he was gay or straight, or whether he would prefer boxers or briefs. He was—if he existed at all—a male. Those of you who remain enamored with the supposed superiority of maleness in the representative figure of our religion can sleep peacefully this evening. But he was more than a male. To use a word of my own invention, Jesus was also *She-sus*. My sincere desire is that this word enter the lexicon of feminist Christology—and soon—before anyone notices how utterly absurd it sounds.

My congregation recently hosted the ordination of Rosemarie Smead as a priest in the Association of Roman Catholic Women Priests (ARCWP), otherwise known as the Association of Women Pain-in-the-Vatican's-Ass Priests. The ARCWP is an offshoot of the larger Roman Catholic Women Priest (RCWP), a movement that began in 2002 on the Danube River when seven women were ordained to the priesthood. My wife and I have become

30. Ibid., 105–6.

friends with some of the women in this movement, including Bishop Mary Bridget Meehan and Janice Sevre-Duszynska. Janice was ordained as a priest in 2008 and spends most of her time agitating at places like the Vatican and the School of the Americas at Fort Benning, Georgia. Her ordination in Lexington, Kentucky, led, four years later, to the excommunication of Roman Catholic Maryknoll priest Roy Bourgeois, the founder of the human rights group School of the Americas Watch (SOA Watch). I think we can all say, without hesitation, that not allowing women to be ordained as priests or ministers or rabbis, or whatever a religion calls their leaders, is beyond ridiculous. Most of the arguments I have heard against women priests usually sound something like this: "Women can't be priests." "Why not?" I ask. "Because women are not allowed to be priests." This makes me proud to be part of the human race.

Dr. Smead's ordination took me back to my Old Testament studies in college where I first learned about Lady Wisdom or *Sophia*. *Sophia* is the Greek word for wisdom, and it just happens to be a feminine noun. By the way, if wisdom is so closely associated with femininity in the ancient traditions then why are our "Wisdom Tables" at places like the local Dairy Queen or McDonalds dominated by older gentlemen? Could it be that what these old geezers are spouting off while drinking coffee, eating sausage biscuits, and bemoaning welfare recipients is not actually wisdom? The Hebrew and Latin words for wisdom, respectively *hochmah* and *sapientia*, are also feminine nouns. The ancients apparently recognized something feminine about wisdom, although they never explain what that is. Wisdom is personified as a woman in places like Proverbs 8 in the Hebrew tradition. I am particularly struck with the following autobiographical statement from Lady Wisdom: "The LORD created me at the beginning of his way, before his deeds long in the past. I was formed in ancient times, at the beginning, before the earth was."[31]

The early Christians knew Jesus was a male and yet they seem to have had no problem connecting Jesus, poetically and theologically, to the one who, according to the Hebrew tradition, helped God in the process of creation: Wisdom. The writer of Colossians, for example, makes a contribution to the link between Jesus and Wisdom by placing Jesus at the beginning of creation: "The son is the image of the invisible God, the one who is first over all creation, because all things were created by him: both in the heavens and on the earth, the things that are visible and the

---

31. Proverbs 8:22–23 (CEB).

things that are invisible. Whether they are thrones or powers, or rulers or authorities, all things were created through him and for him."[32] Is it too obvious to claim that something is obviously going on here? James Robinson suggests that *Sophia* is an "aborted" feminine christological label for Jesus.[33] In addition to the masculine christological terms such as Christ, Lord, Son of God, and Son of Man (all of which are masculine nouns), the early church *could* have inserted a little femininity into the christological language they developed for Jesus. In such a patriarchal society, however, that wasn't going to happen, and yet because we are more enlightened today is there any chance we can add a feminine touch to our Christology without removing Jesus' male member? We won't have to do this unless, of course, our Christology evolves in a way that could only be labeled "Transsexual Christology." Someone should write that book! Still, I think we could do worse than occasionally referring to the dude as *She-sus* . . . as long as I get credit for the word.

More Than the Myth of Redemptive Violence

As I look around today, ears to the ground, nose to the grind, working my fingers to the bone, tongue stuck to the frozen metal pole, my senses tell me that the one thing Jesus is most known for is unfortunately the one thing we need to eliminate from our understanding of him—and from life in general. I'm talking about "the myth of redemptive violence." Most Christians are not familiar with this phrase, first coined by Walter Wink. He argues that "one of the oldest continuously repeated stories in the world" is that violence saves us from further violence, war brings peace, and might makes right.[34] We see the myth everywhere, even in entertainment mediums such as cartoons, movies, television series, and novels. The myth seems very real to us. Wink writes,

> The belief that violence 'saves' is so successful because it doesn't seem to be mythic in the least. Violence simply appears to be the nature of things. It's what works. It seems inevitable, the last and, often, the first resort in conflicts. If a god is what you turn to when all else fails, violence certainly functions as a god. What people

32. Colossians 1:15–16 (CEB).

33. Robinson, "Very Goddess and Very Man: Jesus' Better Self," in Davis, ed., *Encountering Jesus*, 111.

34. Wink, *Powers That Be*, 42.

overlook, then, is the religious character of violence. It demands from its devotees an absolute obedience-unto-death.[35]

It is very common for progressive Christians to bemoan the presence of "redemptive violence" in all its many manifestations today, including war, homicide, terrorism (both domestic and foreign), mass shootings in public places, capital punishment, bullying, spanking, etc.[36] Progressives understand that Jesus was a proponent of nonviolent resistance, if not nonresistance. They understand that in the long run violence doesn't work. It only makes things worse. Violence begets violence. The myth of redemptive violence is usually the prevailing philosophy when a WWII veteran or supporter suggests that the only way to stop Germany and Japan was with brute violent force. Even if that is true—and it is debatable—an exception to a rule doesn't negate the rule. It is still best to err on the side of nonviolence. At the same time, many Christians are not able to apply Jesus' own rejection of the myth of redemptive violence to a theology of the cross. Jesus' violent crucifixion is credited with the redemption of humanity, if not all of creation. This is the view that the only way God could forgive, show mercy, and save humanity was through the violent torture and execution of an innocent man. When one thinks about this, it doesn't make sense, and yet we still cling to it like a tongue on a frozen metal pole. There is a reason why a tongue stuck to a metal pole was featured in the movie *Dumb and Dumber*. The myth of redemptive violence, especially as it is applied to Jesus' violent execution, is *dumberer*.

To say that Jesus is more than the myth of redemptive violence is to say that violence in any form, from world wars to executed sages to spanked bottoms, is not what Jesus was about, and the church that bears his name should refrain from the support of violence *for any reason*. I'm still waiting for the day when the liberal-progressive Christian denominations become part of the "peace church" family. Peace churches are Christian churches, groups, or communities advocating Christian pacifism or biblical nonresistance. The term "historic peace churches" refers specifically only to three church groups among pacifist churches: Church of the Brethren; the Religious Society of Friends (Quakers); and Mennonites, including the Amish, Old Order Mennonite, and Conservative Mennonites.[37] While we

35. Ibid.

36. Claiborne, "Myth of Redemptive Violence."

37. "Peace churches."

are waiting for the mainline churches to come around, I recommend beating your swords into golf clubs (unless you are silly and prefer plowing to golfing).

More Than an Object of Worship

Of course, if a man dies a violent death on a cross for the sins of the world, people will be inclined to worship him as if he is God (or a god). I mean, who wouldn't? This, in a nutshell, is what happened to Jesus. He has become the object of our admiration, veneration, and worship. He has become *Big Jesus*. Is this appropriate? Is this the proper response to the man from Galilee, the one of whom John the Baptist supposedly said, "I'm not even worthy to bend over and loosen the strap of his sandals"?[38] John may not have felt worthy to loosen the straps of a thirty-year-old man's sandals, but if Jesus had lived to be an old fat man it would have been necessary.

Philip Gulley, the popular Quaker minister and writer from Indiana, suggests that worship is *not* our proper response to Jesus. In his wonderfully titled book *If the Church Were Christian*, he first completes that sentence with the startling claim that "Jesus would be a model for living rather than an object of worship." Gulley briefly tells the story of his Catholic upbringing, one that was literally focused on a large crucifix behind the altar. "This Jesus was to be worshipped," he succinctly writes.[39] If Jesus had been Chinese we could just say the crucifixes are *feng shui*. Furthermore, Gulley admits that he believed at the time that the "quality and sincerity" of his worship had a large bearing on where he would spend his eternal destination. And he wasn't talking about Disneyland! He also learned that the proper worship of Jesus included three specific claims about Jesus: 1) his divine origins (virgin birth), 2) his ability to perform miracles, and 3) his sinless nature. Eventually, Gulley learned that these claims are due to the early Christians' inability to speak about their encounter with God through Jesus in any other way. These things confirm his uniqueness, if not his divinity, which merits our adoration.[40]

Almost every Christian church in the world engages in either occasional or frequent worship of Jesus the Christ. This is most obvious in the church's hymnody, ancient or contemporary. Whereas some of the hymns

38. Mark 1:7 (CEB).
39. Gulley, *If the Church Were Christian*, 12.
40. Ibid., 15.

may be less about worship and more about poetic descriptions of Christianity, today's "praise songs" are loaded with adorations of God, Jesus, and the Holy Spirit. Like many of you, I often refer to praise songs as "7-Eleven music" because, you know, there are seven words sung eleven times for the purpose of producing a hypnotic trance in the worshipping community. The other reason praise songs are called "7-Eleven music" is because most of those who engage in such "contemporary worship" come to church with a Big Gulp in hand.

Worship is where the image of Big Jesus is encouraged and sustained. Jesus receives a promotion to divinity each and every weekend. Gulley insists, however, that Jesus would not approve of such accolades. In one of the best articulations of a critique of Big Jesus that I read in all my research for this book, Gulley writes,

> I argue against the deification of Jesus because of my admiration for him. I believe his promotion to divine stature contradicts the Jewish faith of Jesus and ultimately encourages behavior inconsistent with the ethic of Jesus. It has made the church overly proud and prone to asserting itself as the only path to God. In questioning this claim, my wish is not to diminish the life of Jesus, but to honor it as fully as I can by asking whether his elevation to divinity is something he would have wanted.[41]

The alternative is to see Jesus as a model for living, and for those who claim that this somehow diminishes Jesus, Gulley says, "To say Jesus is 'only an example,' as if that were a small thing, underestimates not only the profound difficulty of serving such a role, but also discounts its rarity."[42]

So, Jesus, I'm sorry you had to die on the cross—I truly am—and if I ever have to "take up my cross and follow you," I will gladly do so. (By "gladly" I mean "kicking and screaming.") Still, to be honest with you, I'm much more interested in what you said and did *before* the Romans made an example out of you.

More Than a Survivalist

I know a few people who are paranoid that the government is going to get their guns, especially with a black man in the Oval Office . . . because, you

41. Ibid., 21.
42. Ibid., 24.

know, as soon as the law-abiding white folks lose their guns then the black criminals will easily take over the country, stealing everyone else's welfare checks if not bringing back the institution of white slavery—although good luck finding enough Caucasians that would make good slaves. People also fear that all the bees will soon die and only Monsanto will be able to feed us or that the Russians have already started the nuclear launch codes. None of that is true, except that President Obama is almost certainly coming after your guns and your white daughters . . . which leads to the final point of this book.

In the spirit of Keith Olbermann's "Worst Person in the World" award during his old tenure with MSNBC, which he has revived with his current stint as a funky sportscaster on ESPN, I have concluded that the "Worst Christians in the World" are *paranoid survivalists.* I don't mean those who are paranoid in a mentally ill way. I recognize that sometimes the human brain is at fault. Rather than a mental problem, I'm talking about a *spiritual* problem. There are many models for spirituality bandied about, and I would never be so cocky to claim what is spiritually "good," but I am cocky enough to claim what is spiritually "bad." Our obsessive striving for survival is spiritually bad.

At the same time, however, striving for survival is also a natural human need. Abraham Maslow's hierarchy of human needs begins with our physiological needs, including breathing, food, water, sex, sleep, homeostasis, and excretion. The next level of human needs concern our safety and security, including shelter and having enough resources to survive. All of this is well and good—and natural. Still, given Jesus' willingness to not have a place to rest his head and, more relevant, his willingness to give up his life (not for the bogus notion of human sin, but for his higher principles, which included nonviolence), I suspect that Jesus would have a thing or two to say to the paranoid survivalists in our midst today.

I recently heard John Shelby Spong speak about Jesus' critique of the human quest for survival. As creatures that are self-conscious and aware of our impending deaths, we are naturally obsessed with survival, and yet our obsession can lead to consequences that have the counter-effect of being detrimental to the prospects of our long-term survival. Military spending, including all-too-frequent military action, and our dependence on oil—both of which are deemed necessary for either our survival or our "standard of living"—are good examples of how our spiritually ill obsession with at-all-costs survival is not in the best interests of the longevity of the human race, or all of creation for that matter.

In a very real sense, Jesus was the anti-survivalist. Hear what his following words from the Sermon on the Mount in Matthew's Gospel sound like from that perspective. These are not the words of a gun-toting, cave-dwelling, food-hoarding, money-grubbing American; these are the words of someone who is willing to be exceedingly *vulnerable* to those who may not have his best interests at heart:

- The Beatitudes: Happy are those who are hopeless, who grieve, who are humble, who are hungry and thirsty for righteousness, who show mercy, who have pure hearts, who make peace, and who are harassed. (5:3–10)

- Let your light shine before people. (5:16)

- Turn the other cheek. (5:39)

- If someone asks for your outer garment, give them your inner garment as well. (5:40)

- Give to those who ask, and don't refuse those who wish to borrow from you. (5:42)

- Love your enemies. (5:44)

- Stop collecting treasures for your own benefit on earth. (6:19)

- You cannot serve God and wealth. (6:24)

- Don't worry about your life, what you'll eat or what you'll drink, or what you'll wear. (6:25)

Ironically, Jesus concludes that those who follow his vulnerability-promoting words will find *spiritual survival*: "Everybody who hears these words of mine and puts them into practice is like a wise builder who built a house on bedrock. The rain fell, the floods came, and the wind blew and beat against that house. It didn't fall because it was firmly set on bedrock."[43] In other words, perhaps Jesus' wisdom is beneficial for us *even if the sand is shifting under our feet.*

For those who are more concerned about *physical* survival, my advice is to get some guns and lots of ammunition, build an underground shelter or homestead or a cave, get a guard dog or an elaborate security system, or

43. Matthew 7:24–25 (CEB).

just move to a gated community and hope that if anyone comes after you, it's the black president's minions and *not Big Jesus* . . .

Epic Log

Star Date: 4,570,375,694[1]

FOR FIVE-AND-A-HALF DECADES IN Earth years I have sometimes boldly traveled where only a small percentage of my species has gone. My journey began in semi-desert West Texas surrounded by mesas, mesquite trees, and very large pickup trucks. (I have a theory about why so many Texans drive large pickup trucks and yet I will not share it here. Call me.) I participated in a fair amount of athletic endeavors growing up, particularly baseball, basketball, and golf, only because I grew up in a town so small that one was almost required to play as many sports as one could just so we could field a team. There was also the looming fear of flunking our coach-led science and history classes if we didn't volunteer to play. It is interesting to me that my coaches never taught English. I was not the worst athlete in the world. As a baseball player, I had a glove my dad nicknamed "the suction cup," and in basketball I was occasionally called "the mad bomber," the same nickname one of my daughters would be tagged with in her high school years. (Other than making three-point shots, my daughter was also good at cherry bombing toilets. I'm not at liberty to say which ones.) I was a fair golfer back in the day, playing in the high school state tournament my junior and senior years. In my late teens and early twenties I played fast pitch softball with my dad's team. Dad was a great "stick," rarely striking out, with a proficiency at hitting "Texas leaguers." I still don't know why Texans got to name the hit that lands between infielders and outfielders.

---

1. Believe me when I tell you that this took some fancy calculating on my part.

As a kid I just assumed they named it after my dad. By the way, slow pitch softball is for sissies.

None of the above information about my athletic endeavors is relevant for this book, but a) I have a slight streak of narcissism, and b) I wanted to get this information out there just in case the state of Texas has a hall of fame for skinny athletes who played at least three sports in rural communities and grew up to become United Church of Christ preachers. I'm pretty sure I'm the only one.

I'm not sure, however, that I learned a damn thing about Jesus in those years, yet I do recall the best prayer I ever heard. My little brother's Little League team gathered one night before a big game. The coach asked if anyone would like to pray, which is pretty standard in a culture that prays for safety before Friday night football games. Because of those prayers, every time a player was injured on the field my faith plummeted like the 1929 stock market. On this occasion, however, no one volunteered until the biggest badass on the field said, "I will, coach." I was standing near the players and the sound of this young man volunteering to pray was enough to distract me from the smell of leather gloves and fresh popcorn. I'll never forget his prayer: "Dear Lord, thank you for *everything*."

And just like that I was introduced to Big Jesus . . . because that's who Jesus has become in a culture that is obsessed with personal salvation, the prosperity gospel, and all the other hyper-narcissistic theologies we can imagine. Jesus has become our *everything*:

> You are my everything,
> You are the song I sing;
> I'll do anything for you
> Teach me how to pray,
> To live a life of grace;
> I'll go anywhere with you
> Jesus, be my everything.[2]

Jesus, as God's stand-in, has become everything to a lot of people. Well, not *everything*. When I mow my grass I don't think to myself, "Jesus, you are my lawn guy!" It would be awesome to tell people that Jesus is my lawn guy but they would just assume I was talking about a Mexican guy. Still, in his name we pray that high school football players will be kept safe from injury, people in hospital beds will receive healing, drought-stricken land

---

2. Matt Maher, "Jesus, My Everything," from his album *Welcome to Life* (2005).

will receive rain, and dead car batteries will come back to life. Jesus has become our culture's relationship guru, our model for leadership, and the one we follow even though most of us don't know (and don't care) where his path would actually lead us.

I have not written this book to burst anyone's bubble about Jesus. I suspect that will happen sooner or later to most people. Instead, I have written this book on *behalf* of Jesus, who spoke to me one day and said,

> Please, Jimmy, tell people to chill. I don't mind them singing about me or even talking to me before they go to bed. I don't mind that they have built a few statues of me, or painted a lot of pictures of me looking all European. I don't even mind that a few of them think they have seen my image on an old shroud, in a slice of bread, in cloud formations, or in yellow snow. [I once saw the European Jesus in the snow after my dog relieved himself. Miracle? Canine penile artistry? You tell me.] I'm not too bothered that they think I can heal their loved ones or help them get a better job—as long as they go to the doctor and conduct a professional job interview. But this high Christology stuff, man, dude, it's sort of for the birds. I mean, how can I live up to that? This is too much pressure.

Jesus really didn't say all of that to me. I made up the shroud thing because, curiously, he seems to have forgotten all about that.

Well, that about does it for me. I really don't have anything else to say. Also, I have to write a sermon for Sunday, create a bulletin, visit the shut-ins, go to a meeting or two, feed my dog, do some laundry, walk my dog, get on the treadmill, read something, talk to my wife . . .

Bibliography

Anderson, Ray S. *An Emergent Theology for Emerging Churches*. Downers Grove, IL: InterVarsity, 2006.

Armstrong, Karen, et al. *The Once & Future Faith*. Santa Rosa, CA: Polebridge, 2001.

Axtell, James. "History as Imagination." *The Historian* 49/4 (August 1987) 451–62.

Aylesworth, Gary. "Postmodernism." *Stanford Encyclopedia of Philosophy*. Online: http://plato.stanford.edu/entries/postmodernism/.

"Bad-Ass Jesus." Faithfool. July 14, 2007. Online: http://faithfool.wordpress.com/2007/07/14/bad-ass-jesus/.

Baker, Mark D., editor. *Proclaiming the Scandal of the Cross: Contemporary Images of the Atonement*. Grand Rapids: Baker, 2006.

Bakker, Jay, with Martin Edlund. *Fall to Grace: A Revolution of God, Self, & Society*. New York: FaithWords, 2011.

Bass, Diana Butler. *A People's History of Christianity: The Other Side of the Story*. New York: HarperOne, 2009.

Batterson, Mark. *Wild Goose Chase: Reclaim the Adventure of Pursuing God*. Colorado Springs, CO: Multnomah, 2008.

Beacon, R., Jr. "The Unwritten Things which Jesus Did." *The Bible Treasury* 18 (1891). Online: http://stempublishing.com/magazines/bt/BT18/1891_347_Unwritten_Things_Jesus_Did.html.

Bell, Rob. *Love Wins: A Book about Heaven, Hell, and the Fate of Every Person Who Ever Lived*. New York: HarperOne, 2011.

———. *What We Talk about When We Talk about God*. New York: HarperOne, 2013.

Bessler, Joseph A. *A Scandalous Jesus: How Three Historic Quests Changed Theology for the Better*. Salem, OR: Polebridge, 2013.

Bessler-Northcutt, Joe, et al. *The Historical Jesus Goes to Church*. Santa Rosa, CA: Polebridge, 2004.

Borg, Marcus J. *Jesus, a New Vision: Spirit, Culture, and the Life of Discipleship*. San Francisco: Harper & Row, 1987.

———, editor. *Jesus at 2000*. Boulder, CO: Westview, 1998.

———. *Jesus in Contemporary Scholarship*. Valley Forge, PA: Trinity, 1994.

———. *Jesus: Uncovering the Life, Teachings, and Relevance of a Religious Revolutionary*. San Francisco: HarperSanFrancisco, 2006.

———. *Meeting Jesus Again for the First Time: The Historical Jesus & the Heart of Contemporary Faith*. San Francisco: HarperSanFrancisco, 1994.

———. *The Heart of Christianity: Rediscovering a Life of Faith.* San Francisco: HarperSanFrancisco, 2003.

Borg, Marcus J., and N. T. Wright. *The Meaning of Jesus: Two Visions.* San Francisco: HarperSanFrancisco, 1999.

Bourgeault, Cynthia. *The Wisdom Jesus: Transforming Heart and Mind: A New Perspective on Christ and His Message.* Boston: Shambhala, 2008.

Brown, Raymond Edward. *An Introduction to New Testament Christology.* New York: Paulist, 1994.

Burchfiel, Nathan. "'Progressive' Christians Say Media Coverage Skewed to Religious Right." CNSNews.com, May 31, 2007. Online: http://www.christianheadlines.com/news/progressive-christians-say-media-coverage-skewed-to-religious-right-11542652.html.

Carr, Jeremy. "How Tall Was Jesus?" One Thing. April 25, 2012. Online: http://jeremyacarr.blogspot.com/2010/09/how-tall-was-jesus.html.

Chalke, Steve, and Alan Mann. *The Lost Message of Jesus.* Grand Rapids: Zondervan, 2003.

Chilton, Bruce. *Rabbi Jesus: An Intimate Biography.* New York: Doubleday, 2000.

"Circular reasoning." Wikipedia. Online: http://en.wikipedia.org/wiki/Circular_reasoning.

Claiborne, Shane. "The Myth of Redemptive Violence." *Huffington Post,* July 23, 2012. Online: http://www.huffingtonpost.com/shane-claiborne/myth-of-redemptive-violence_b_1695889.html.

Claiborne, Shane, and Tony Campolo. *Red Letter Revolution: What If Jesus Really Meant What He Said?* Nashville: Thomas Nelson, 2012.

Cobb, John B. *The Process Perspective: Frequently Asked Questions about Process Theology.* St. Louis: Chalice, 2003.

Copan, Paul, editor. *Will the Real Jesus Please Stand Up?: A Debate between William Lane Craig and John Dominic Crossan.* Grand Rapids: Baker, 1998.

Crossan, John Dominic. *God and Empire: Jesus against Rome, Then and Now.* New York: HarperOne, 2007.

———. *The Historical Jesus: The Life of a Mediterranean Jewish Peasant.* San Franscisco: Harper, 1991.

———. *Jesus: A Revolutionary Biography.* San Francisco: HarperSanFrancisco, 1994.

———. *The Power of Parable: How Fiction by Jesus Became Fiction about Jesus.* New York: HarperOne, 2012.

Crossan, John Dominic, and Jonathan L. Reed. *Excavating Jesus: Beneath the Stones, Behind the Texts.* New York: HarperOne, 2001.

Cupitt, Don. *Reforming Christianity.* Santa Rosa, CA: Polebridge, 2001.

Daniel, Lillian. *When "Spiritual but Not Religious" Is Not Enough: Seeing God in Surprising Places, Even the Church.* New York: Jericho, 2013.

"Cyrus the Great." Wikipedia. Online: http://en.wikipedia.org/wiki/Cyrus_the_Great.

Daniel, Prayson. "Busting the Dying and Rising Gods Myths." With All I Am. May 28, 2011. Online: http://withalliamgod.wordpress.com/2011/05/28/busting-the-dying-and-rising-gods-myths/.

Davis, Stephen T., editor. *Encountering Jesus: A Debate on Christology.* Atlanta: John Knox, 1988.

Dawes, Gregory W., editor. *The Historical Jesus Quest: Landmarks in the Search for the Jesus of History.* Louisville: Westminster John Knox, 1999.

Ehrman, Bard D. *Jesus, Apocalyptic Prophet of the New Millennium.* New York: Oxford University Press, 1999.

———. *Misquoting Jesus: The Story Behind Who Changed the Bible and Why.* San Francisco: HarperSanFrancisco, 2005.

"Emerging church." Wikipedia. Online: http://en.wikipedia.org/wiki/Emerging_church.

Enns, Peter. "Were David Koresh and the Branch Dividians Guilty of Plagiarism?" Patheos. April 20, 2013. Online: http://www.patheos.com/blogs/peterenns/2013/04/were-david-koresh-and-the-branch-dividians-guilty-of-plagiarism/.

Felten, David M., and Jeff Procter-Murphy. *Living the Questions: The Wisdom of Progressive Christianity.* New York: HarperOne, 2012.

Fox, Richard Wightman. *Jesus in America: Personal Savior, Cultural Hero, National Obsession.* San Francisco: HarperSanFrancisco, 2004.

Funk, Robert Walter. *A Credible Jesus: Fragments of a Vision.* Santa Rosa, CA: Polebridge, 2002.

———. *Honest to Jesus: Jesus for a New Millennium.* San Francisco: HarperSanFrancisco, 1996.

———. *Jesus as Precursor.* Rev. ed. Sonoma, CA: Polebridge, 1994.

Funk, Robert Walter, Roy W. Hoover, and the Jesus Seminar. *The Five Gospels: The Search for the Authentic Words of Jesus.* New York: Macmillan, 1993.

Galston, David. *Embracing the Human Jesus: A Wisdom Path for Contemporary Christianity.* Salem, OR: Polebridge, 2012.

Geering, Lloyd George. *Christianity without God.* Santa Rosa, CA: Polebridge, 2002.

Gellene, Denise. "Study Finds Left-Wing Brain, Right-Wing Brain." *Los Angeles Times,* September 10, 2007. Online: http://articles.latimes.com/2007/sep/10/science/la-sci-politics10sep10.

Gibbs, Eddie, and Ryan K. Bolger. *Emerging Churches: Creating Christian Community in Postmodern Cultures.* Grand Rapids: Baker Academic, 2005.

Gibson, Greg. "God Is Too Big to Fit into One Religion." May 12, 2010. Online: http://ggib.me/2010/05/12/god-is-too-big-to-fit-into-one-religion/.

Gladwell, Malcolm. *Outliers: The Story of Success.* New York: Little, Brown, 2008.

"Gov. Rick Perry: 'Freedom of religion doesn't mean freedom from religion.'" June 13, 2013. Online: http://www.examiner.com/article/gov-rick-perry-freedom-of-religion-doesn-t-mean-freedom-from-religion.

Gulley, Philip. *If the Church Were Christian: Rediscovering the Values of Jesus.* New York: HarperOne, 2010.

Hedrick, Charles W., editor. *When Faith Meets Reason: Religion Scholars Reflect on Their Spiritual Journeys.* Santa Rosa, CA: Polebridge, 2008.

Heyward, Carter. *Saving Jesus from Those Who Are Right: Rethinking What It Means to Be Christian.* Minneapolis: Fortress, 1999.

Hoover, Roy W., editor. *Profiles of Jesus.* Santa Rosa, CA: Polebridge, 2002.

Hume, David. *An Enquiry Concerning Human Understanding.* Harvard Classics 37/3. New York: P. F. Collier, 1909–14. Online: http://www.bartleby.com/37/3/.

The Jesus Seminar. *The Once and Future Jesus.* Santa Rosa, CA: Polebridge, 2000.

"John Shelby Spong." Wikipedia. Online: http://en.wikipedia.org/wiki/John_Shelby_Spong.

Jones, Tony. *A Better Atonement: Beyond the Depraved Doctrine of Original Sin.* Kindle ebook. Jopa Group, 2012.

———. *The New Christians: Dispatches from the Emergent Frontier.* San Francisco: Jossey-Bass, 2008.

Kaczynski, Andrew. "Is This the Most Embarrassing Interview Fox News Has Ever Done?" July 27, 2013. Online: http://www.buzzfeed.com/andrewkaczynski/is-this-the-most-embarrassing-interview-fox-news-has-ever-do.

Kimball, Dan. *The Emerging Church: Vintage Christianity for New Generations.* Grand Rapids: Zondervan, 2003.

Kinniman, David, and Gabe Lyons. *Unchristian: What a New Generation Really Thinks about Christianity—and Why It Matters.* Grand Rapids: Baker, 2007.

Kübler-Ross, Elisabeth. *On Death and Dying: What the Dying Have to Teach Doctors, Nurses, Clergy and Their Own Families.* 40th anniversary ed. New York: Routledge, 2009.

Laughlin, Paul Alan, and Glenna S. Jackson. *Remedial Christianity: What Every Believer Should Know about the Faith, but Probably Doesn't.* Santa Rosa, CA: Polebridge, 2000.

Leong, Kenneth S. *The Zen Teachings of Jesus.* Rev. ed. New York: Crossroad, 2001.

Levine, Amy-Jill. *The Misunderstood Jew: The Church and the Scandal of the Jewish Jesus.* New York: HarperOne, 2006.

Martin, Raymond. *The Elusive Messiah: A Philosophical Overview of the Quest for the Historical Jesus.* Boulder, CO: Westview, 2000.

McKnight, Scot. "Five Streams of the Emerging Church." *Christianity Today,* February 2007. Online: http://www.christianitytoday.com/ct/2007/february/11.35.html.

McLaren, Brian D. *Everything Must Change: When the World's Biggest Problems and Jesus' Good News Collide.* Nashville: Thomas Nelson, 2007.

———. *A Generous Orthodoxy: Why I Am a Missional, Evangelical, Post/Protestant, Liberal/Conservative, Mystical/Poetic, Biblical, Charismatic/Contemplative, Fundamentalist/Calvinist, Anabaptist/Anglican, Methodist, Catholic, Green, Incarnational, Depressed-yet-Hopeful, Emergent, Unfinished Christian.* Grand Rapids: Zondervan, 2004.

———. *A New Kind of Christian: A Tale of Two Friends on a Spiritual Journey.* San Francisco: Jossey-Bass, 2001.

———. *A New Kind of Christianity: Ten Questions That Are Transforming the Faith.* New York: HarperOne, 2010.

———. *The Secret Message of Jesus: Uncovering the Truth That Could Change Everything.* Nashville: W. Publishing, 2006.

———. *Why Did Jesus, Moses, the Buddha, and Mohammed Cross the Road?: Christian Identity in a Multi-Faith World.* New York: Jericho, 2012.

McLaren, Brian D., and Tony Campolo. *Adventures in Missing the Point: How the Culture-Controlled Church Neutered the Gospel.* Grand Rapids: Zondervan, 2003.

McLennan, Scotty. *Jesus Was a Liberal: Reclaiming Christianity for All.* New York: Palgrave Macmillan, 2009.

Mesle, C. Robert. *Process Theology: A Basic Introduction.* St. Louis: Chalice, 1993.

Meyers, Robin. *The Underground Church: Reclaiming the Subversive Way of Jesus.* San Francisco: Jossey-Bass, 2012.

Miller, Robert J. *The Jesus Seminar and Its Critics.* Santa Rosa, CA: Polebridge, 1999.

Morwood, Michael. *Is Jesus God?: Finding Our Faith.* New York: Crossroad, 2001.

"Napoleon complex." *Wikipedia.* Online: vhttp://en.wikipedia.org/wiki/Napoleon_complex.

Nelson-Pallmeyer, Jack. *Jesus Against Christianity: Reclaiming the Missing Jesus.* Harrisburg, PA: Trinity, 2001.

"A New Christianity for a New World." Wikipedia. Online: http://en.wikipedia.org/wiki/A_New_Christianity_for_a_New_World.

Nolan, Albert. *Jesus Before Christianity*. Maryknoll, NY: Orbis, 1996.

———. *Jesus Today: A Spirituality of Radical Freedom*. Maryknoll, NY: Orbis, 2006.

Pagitt, Doug. *A Christianity Worth Believing: Hope-Filled, Open-Armed, Alive-and-Well Faith for the Left Out, Left Behind, and Let Down in Us All*. San Francisco: Jossey-Bass, 2008.

Pagitt, Doug, and Tony Jones, editors. *An Emergent Manifesto of Hope*. Grand Rapids: Baker, 2007.

"Peace churches." Wikipedia. Online: http://en.wikipedia.org/wiki/Peace_churches.

Pelikan, Jaroslav. *Jesus through the Centuries: His Place in the History of Culture*. New York: Harper & Row, 1985.

Pinker, Steven. *The Better Angels of Our Nature: Why Violence Has Declined*. New York: Viking, 2011.

Plantinga, Alvin. "Spiritual Autobiography." University of Notre Dame, March 1992. Online: http://www.calvin.edu/125th/wolterst/p_bio.pdf

Powell, Mark Allan. *Jesus as a Figure in History: How Modern Historians View the Man from Galilee*. Louisville: Westminster John Knox, 1998.

"Process theology." Wikipedia. Online: http://en.wikipedia.org/wiki/Process_theology.

Prothero, Stephen R. *American Jesus: How the Son of God Became a National Icon*. New York: Farrar, Straus and Giroux, 2003.

Rice, Anne. "Reasons for Quitting Christianity." Online: http://www.annerice.com/Chamber-Christianity.html.

Robinson, James M. *A New Quest of the Historical Jesus and Other Essays*. Philadelphia: Fortress, 1983.

Sanders, E. P. *The Historical Figure of Jesus*. New York: Penguin, 1993.

———. *Jesus and Judaism*. Minneapolis: Fortress, 1985.

Sandlin, Mark. "Superman vs. Jesus." *Huffington Post*, June 14, 2013. Online: http://www.huffingtonpost.com/mark-sandlin/superman-vs-jesus_b_3444361.html.

Schwartzentruber, Michael, editor. *The Emerging Christian Way: Thoughts, Stories, and Wisdom for a Faith of Transformation*. Kelowna, BC: CopperHouse, 2006.

Schweitzer, Albert. *The Quest of the Historical Jesus: A Critical Study of Its Progress from Reimarus to Wrede*. Translated by W. Montgomery. New York: Macmillan, 1968.

Scott, Bernard Brandon. *Re-Imagine the World: An Introduction to the Parables of Jesus*. Santa Rosa, CA: Polebridge, 2001.

"7 Big Questions." *Relevant*, January/February 2007. Online: http://web.archive.org/web/20071013102203/http://relevantmagazine.com/god_article.php?id=7418.

Sheehan, Thomas. *The First Coming: How the Kingdom of God Became Christianity*. New York: Random House, 1986.

Smith, Huston. "Do Drugs Have Religious Import?" *Journal of Philosophy* 61/18 (September 1964).

Snider, Phil, editor. *The Hyphenateds: How Emergence Christianity is Re-Traditioning Mainline Practices*. St. Louis: Chalice, 2011.

Spong, John Shelby. *Jesus for the Non-Religious: Recovering the Divine at the Heart of the Human*. New York: HarperOne, 2007.

———. *Liberating the Gospels: Reading the Bible with Jewish Eyes: Freeing Jesus from 2,000 Years of Misunderstanding*. San Francisco: HarperSanFrancisco, 1996.

———. *A New Christianity for a New World: Why Traditional Faith Is Dying and How a New Faith Is Being Born*. San Francisco: HarperSanFrancisco, 2001.

———. *Rescuing the Bible from Fundamentalism: A Bishop Rethinks the Meaning of Scripture*. San Francisco: HarperSanFrancisco, 1991.

———. *Resurrection: Myth or Reality?: A Bishop's Search for the Origins of Christianity*. San Francisco: HarperSanFrancisco, 1994.

———. *Why Christianity Must Change or Die: A Bishop Speaks to Believers in Exile: A New Reformation of the Church's Fath and Practice*. San Francisco: HarperSanFrancisco, 1998.

Stewart, Robert B., editor. *The Resurrection of Jesus: John Dominic Crossan and N.T. Wright in Dialogue*. Minneapolis: Fortress, 2006.

"Study Finds Fox News Viewers Least Informed of All Viewers." *Huffington Post*, May 23, 2012. Online: http://www.huffingtonpost.com/2012/05/23/fox-news-less-informed-new-study_n_1538914.html.

Sullivan, Clayton. *Rescuing Jesus from the Christians*. Harrisburg, PA: Trinity, 2002.

Thielen, Martin. *What's the Least I Can Believe and Still Be a Christian?: A Guide to What Matters Most*. Louisville: Westminster John Knox, 2011.

Tickle, Phyllis. *Emergence Christianity: What It Is, Where It Is Going, and Why It Matters*. Grand Rapids: Baker, 2012.

———. *The Great Emergence: How Christianity Is Changing and Why*. Grand Rapids: Baker, 2008.

"Too big to fail." Wikipedia. Online: http://en.wikipedia.org/wiki/Too_big_to_fail.

Webber, Robert. *Ancient-Future Worship: Proclaiming and Enacting God's Narrative*. Grand Rapids: Baker, 2008.

———, editor. *Listening to the Beliefs of Emerging Churches: Five Perspectives*. Grand Rapids: Zondervan, 2007.

Wellman, James K., Jr. *Rob Bell and a New American Christianity*. Nashville: Abingdon, 2012.

Wink, Walter. *The Powers That Be: Theology for a New Millennium*. New York: Doubleday, 1998.

Wright, N. T., and John Dominic Crossan. *The Resurrection of Jesus: John Dominic Crossan and N.T. Wright in Dialogue*. Edited by Robert B. Stewart. Minneapolis: Fortress, 2006.

Made in the USA
San Bernardino, CA
07 December 2016